BARBARA ADOLF & KAROL ROSE

THE EMPLOYER'S GUIDE TO CHILD CARE

Developing Programs for Working Parents

Second Edition, Revised and Expanded

BARBARA ADOLF

PRAEGER

New York
Westport, Connecticut
London

Library of Congress Cataloging-in-Publication Data

Adolf, Barbara.
    The employer's guide to child care.

    Bibliography: p.
    Includes index.
    1. Employer-supported day care—United States.
2. Day care centers and industry—United States.
3. Day care centers—United States—Evaluation.
I. Rose, Karol. II. Title.
HF5549.5.D39A36   1988   658.3'8   88-2343
ISBN 0-275-92891-8 (alk. paper)

Library of Congress Catalog Card Number: 88-2343

ISBN: 0-275-92891-8

First published in 1988

Praeger Publishers, One Madison Avenue, New York, NY 10010
A division of Greenwood Press, Inc.

Printed in the United States of America

∞

The paper used in this book complies with the
Permanent Paper Standard issued by the National
Information Standards Organization (Z39.48-1984).

10 9 8 7 6 5 4 3 2

THE EMPLOYER'S GUIDE TO CHILD CARE

To Gerry

CONTENTS

WORKSHEETS AND TABLES

PREFACE

In the three years since the first edition was published, much has happened:

- Individual stories of the dilemmas of working families have appeared in newspapers, magazines, and on television, heightening public awareness of the profound changes in work and family that have affected our society.
- Corporations, unions, and government entities are now concerned that inadequate child care and work policies present dangers to children and employees. These corporate leaders have begun to commit time and resources to change their policies and behaviors.
- New research that quantifies the problem is helping define why and how change must take place. Much of the data reinforce the work of those of us who have been practitioners in the field over the last ten years.

The field of employer-supported child care has grown and changed. As the spheres of work and family continue to affect one another, employer-supported child care will continue to evolve. This book addresses that process. It attempts to break the field into manageable pieces, so that any employer can begin to deal successfully with the real needs of his or her own work force. Employers who are already involved with support programs can also benefit from the book; the information and worksheets can be used to evaluate existing programs and answer the question, "Where do I go from here?"

Karol Rose and I have moved from our joint effort into new realms, separate yet related to employer support for working parents. Karol, a management trainer at Time Inc., is helping develop and implement corporate policy that responds to the needs of working families. I, as associate benefit consultant with Buck Consultants, continue to work with employers throughout the country, helping them assess, design, and implement employer-supported child and elder care programs. I am able to present employer-supported child care as one aspect of employee family needs within the broader context of employee benefits, compensation, and personnel policies.

What Karol and I began in the first edition I am continuing in the second. My intent is to add new insights to the base of practical information and to continue to help employers solve the family/work dilemma. My mission seems especially urgent now.

INTRODUCTION

The increasing presence of women in the work force is causing major changes in U.S. family life, in the roles women and men play at work and at home, and in the way children are being raised. Corporations are rethinking the relationship between work life and home life, recognizing that work and family can no longer be considered separate.

As companies grapple with identifying and responding to the family needs of their employees, they require information and professional guidance—to understand what their options are, what these will cost, and what they have to gain or lose by choosing one option over another.

This book is designed for business professionals. Each section provides information and relevant worksheets about a specific phase of employer involvement. Using the worksheets, you can develop a report documenting the needs, identifying the options, and outlining the process for decision making. Information is included to help you identify high-quality child care, which is essential to any employer-supported program.

Whether your consultant only assists you in certain phases of the study or conducts the entire study for you, you will want to understand the process involved. The book will provide a practical overview of the complex field of employer-supported child care, enabling you to make informed decisions for your company.

THE EMPLOYER'S GUIDE TO CHILD CARE

1

WHO'S WORKING?

A major Eastern high-tech company was faced with a problem. The company had had its most successful year ever, and profits were way up, but several of its best paid professionals—scientists and executives—had recently left to join competitors. Why did they leave? Surprisingly, higher pay was not the main reason. Exit interviews revealed that employees were joining companies that offered better family benefits such as more days off, and, in one case, a high-quality child care center for the employees' children.

In the majority of cases, employees who left had working spouses and young children. They reported that finding quality child care was one of their most difficult problems. They reasoned that any company that showed sensitivity to this problem could probably be counted on to support its employees through other personal problems they might encounter.

A look at the demographics of the total employee population revealed that nearly half of the workers were female, up from about one-quarter only a few years earlier. Also, nearly three-quarters were in their child bearing years, between the ages of 21 and 40.

Throughout the company, employees frequently talked about the difficulty of managing their families while they worked. Professionally conducted "focus groups" with employees revealed that those with older children worried about leaving them unsupervised after school. Those with younger children worried that the care their children were getting was not "stimulating" enough. Some parents worried that they might not even recognize a harmful child care arrangement.

A professional study helped the company take a close look at its employees' child care needs. After examining the feasibility of a child care center at the largest site (which served 2,000 employees), it was decided to develop a program primarily for infants. The plan was to "start small" and, when and if appropriate, add a school-age program. Other services were developed—resource and referral, workshops, and some written materials.

This company's experience is not unique. Today, women make up more than 45 percent of the work force in this country, a threefold increase since 1940. In recent years, nearly two-thirds of entrants to the work force have been women.[1] In the same period, the number of working mothers has gone up ten times.[2] In 1987, more than 60 percent of the mothers of children under 18 (33 million mothers) were working.[3] By 1995, 80 percent of women between the ages of 25 and 44 will be working and 90 percent of these working women will be raising babies at some point during their work lives.[4]

This change in the composition of the work force and in motherhood (and fatherhood) has been gathering momentum steadily since World War II. Some see it as a social revolution. However, it has also been called the "subtle revolution," because U.S. business has been slow to acknowledge the change.

The fact is, U.S. society has undergone a radical transformation in the post-1945 era: a transformation of its most basic support structure, the family. Only one in ten U.S. families fits the traditional pattern of a breadwinner father with a

Table 1
Percent of Mothers in the Work Force
by Age of Youngest Child

Age of Youngest Child	1977	1982	1987
1 Year or Younger	36.6%	43.3%	51.9%
2 Years	42.2%	52.0%	58.0%
3 Years	45.9%	56.4%	60.4%
4 Years	48.8%	56.0%	62.4%
5 Years	50.6%	57.4%	63.1%

Source: Bureau of Labor Statistics, March 1987.

wife at home. In 59 percent of husband/wife families with children the wife works, up from 45 percent just ten years ago.[5] One of every four families with children is headed by a woman.[6]

The mothers of more than half of all children under three are working.[7] These women make up the fastest growing segment of the labor force. Even more startling is that half of all mothers with children under age one are working or looking for work (compared with 38 percent in 1980 and 31 percent in 1976).[8]

Of working women who give birth, 50 percent return to their jobs soon after delivery.[9] Table 1 shows the percentage of working mothers by the age of their youngest child.

WHY MOTHERS WORK

Studies show that women work for the same reasons men do—for the satisfaction it gives them and, a more pressing reason, because they need the money. Of married women, about 40 percent have husbands who earn less than $15,000 per year.[10] These women work not for luxuries, like a second car or a family vacation, but to keep their families out of debt.

The United States has the highest divorce rate in the world. Almost 13 million children (1 in every 5 in the United States) live with single mothers who are the sole breadwinners in their households.[11] The number of single-parent households had grown to almost 9 million in 1985.[12] In 1984, the median income for single-parent families was $12,803, while for married families with 2 children it was $25,338.[13] In 1984, 1 in 3 single-mother families lived below the poverty level compared with 1 in 14 other families.[14]

At the same time that the role of women has been changing, there have been other profound transformations in U.S. society. Our population is increasingly mobile. Family members are no longer as likely to live near one another. The extended family of aunts and uncles, cousins, and grandparents no longer acts as a support system for many working parents, and when these relatives are nearby, they are less available to care for children because many of them are also working.

CHANGING ATTITUDES

Research shows that many workers today consider their family responsibilities primary.[15] A study commissioned by *Fortune Magazine* found that two out of five working parents surveyed felt that work interferes with family life. One-fifth of the fathers and more than one-quarter of the mothers were looking for a job that was less demanding in order to have more time with their families.

Fathers were even more affected than mothers. One in three, compared with one in four mothers, had actually refused a job promotion or transfer because it would have meant less time with their families.[16] This increased concern by fathers with working wives has been corroborated by a Stanford University study of dual-MBA couples.

HOW CHILDREN OF WORKING PARENTS ARE CARED FOR

A study by the U.S. Census Bureau found that of the more than 8 million children under age 5 with working mothers, the largest group—37 percent—are cared for in someone else's home. Thirty-one percent are cared for in their own homes. Nearly one-quarter are cared for in a child care center or nursery school, up from 16 percent in 1982.

The children of full-time working mothers are even more likely to be cared for outside the home than the children of part-time working mothers (75 to 68 percent). Twenty-four percent of children whose mothers work part-time (evenings or weekends) are cared for by their fathers, compared with 11 percent whose mothers work full time.

Of the 18 million school-age children whose parents work, the majority need care after school.[17] One survey found that about one-third of these children have another arrangement in addition to school while their parents work. Slightly more than 2 million are cared for in their own homes and 1.3 million are cared for in someone else's home. Only a little more than 300,000 children are cared for in organized before- or after-school group programs, although many parents say that they would prefer such programs if they were available.[18]

Accurate figures are hard to obtain, but anywhere between 2.5 and 15 million children ages 5 to 13 years care for themselves at least some part of the workday.[19] These children are sometimes referred to as "latchkey" children because of the house keys they carry around their necks. While older children are more likely to be caring for themselves (more than one-fifth of 12- and 13-year-olds), one survey found that 16 percent of children 9 to 11 years are in self-care, as are 6 percent of 5- to 8-year-olds whose mothers work full time. While about one-third of the children were reported to be left alone for less than an hour, 1 in 10 were without adult supervision for three hours or more.[20]

GOVERNMENT AND CHILD CARE

Unlike most industrialized countries, the United States lacks an organized system of child care services that meet the changing needs of families. In the past, the federal government had set some standards to monitor child care, but recent budget cuts have curtailed these activities. Responsibility for child care has shifted to the states. While some states have begun to examine their child care policies and increase funding for programs, in 1986, 29 states actually withdrew support.[21]

The vast majority of child care in this country is unlicensed, unregulated, and "underground." For example, there are about 1.75 million family day care homes in the United States, 9 out of 10 of which are neither licensed nor registered. Nevertheless, 40 percent of all infants and toddlers whose mothers work are cared for in these homes.[22]

Child care workers are among the lowest paid workers in our society, with an average salary of $9,000 per year. Consequently, their turnover rate is 42 percent, one of the highest of any job in the United States.[23]

Ironically, organized and monitored quality child care is hardest to find for those with the greatest need—infants and toddlers. The lack of services is also acute for young school-age children who may need supervision to get to and from school safely, and after school. Some of these children are anxious about being alone. Up to now, little has been done to help parents provide their children with a safe, supervised experience.[24]

Frequently, a working parent must arrange for several different types of child care and for transportation from one program to another. When the child or caregiver is sick, the parent must find back-up care. In her study of working mothers, Sheila Kamerman found that some parents made use of as many as six child care arrangements in one week. These have been termed child care "packages." If one piece is out of place, the whole package often falls apart.[25]

WHAT CHILD CARE COSTS

In 1984, the median cost of child care for women with one child was $39 per week. Twenty-five percent paid $50 or more per week.[26] Costs can go as high as $350 per week for care in the child's own home (such care tends to be most expensive). Family day care (child care in someone else's home) is usually less expensive. Child care centers charge between $40 and $200 per week per child depending on the locale (care in cities tends to be more costly than in rural areas) and the age of the child (care for younger children tends to be more costly than for older children).

For example, in central New Jersey, these are the weekly costs of family day care and child center care as of June 1986.[27]

Category	Mean	Median	Range
Infants	$82.50	$82.50	$65–$100
Child care: 2½ to 6 yrs.	$56.38	$57.00	$30–$80

Since women earn about two-thirds of what men do, single mothers tend to have the most difficulty in meeting child care costs. The average single mother earns approximately $12,000 per year. If care for her child costs $3,000, this will mean that one-quarter of her income must go to child care. If she has more than one child, the cost may be prohibitive. It is not unusual for parents earning $25,000 a year to pay a large portion of their income for child care, especially if they have more than one child. Table 2 shows the relative costs of child care in major cities throughout the United States.

Table 2
Cost of Child Care per Week in Seven Cities, January 1985,
for Children under Five

	Family Day Care	Center Care	School-Age Program	In Child's Own Home
Boston	$45-160	$75-150	$30-40	$260-340
New York	$35-140	$50-150	$20-60	$165-300
Atlanta	$30- 60	$50-150	$20-35	$165-230
St. Louis	$35- 50	$50-80	$10-32	$165 and up
Dallas	$50- 70	$50-90	$25-35	$165-200
Denver	$55- 105	$55-105	$30	$165-200
San Francisco	$55-90	$65-120	___	$165-200

Source: Dana Friedman, *Corporate Financial Assistance for Child Care*, New York: The Conference Board, 1985, 7.

NOT JUST A WOMEN'S ISSUE

Research shows that today most men whose wives work share the child care responsibilities and the anxiety. Nearly half of the men in the *Fortune Magazine* study reported feeling stressed and anxious over the past three months because of child care arrangements.[28] Enlightened employers recognize that child care problems affect families, not just women.

HOW EMPLOYERS CAN RESPOND

In 1980, the White House Conference on Families predicted:

Even companies that employ few, if any, women will come under pressure to initiate family oriented policies on behalf of their male workers. For it is increasingly likely today that these men are married to working women and such issues as flextime, child care and paternity leave...apply equally to their family needs and responsibilities.[29]

Business organizations, chambers of commerce, and professional groups are providing forums for studying the needs of working parents. Many states have

Worksheet 1
Composition of the Work Force

Try to estimate figures for each of these categories. Use medical claims data and other personnel records for rough estimates. This will help you identify groups needing child care assistance.

<u>number</u>   <u>med salary</u>*   <u>% of workforce</u>

1. Employees by job category
e.g. Clerical
     Professional
     Technical

2. Female employees
between 20 and 40 yrs
old (by job category)

3. Male employees
between 20 and 40 yrs
old (by job category)

4. Married employees
between 20 and 40

5. Single employees
between 20 and 40

6. Employees with
dependents under 6 yrs

7. Employees with
dependents 6–14 yrs

8. Employees who are
single parents

9. Employees with a
wage earning spouse
and at least 1 child

*Note that this does not take into account spouse and other family income.

Worksheet 2
Sample Problems of Working Parents

Talk with individual employees to get anecdotal information about the types of problems and how these impact on work.

Job Category	Child Care Problem	Effect on Work	Cost to Company
e.g. Engineer	lack of quality infant care	anxious, leaves work 1.5 hrs/wk early	1.5 hrs/wk@25/hr. = $1,800/yr.

Worksheet 3
Cost of Child Care for Employees

Ten % of an employee's income is considered reasonable for child care. Even after an employee takes the standard tax credit, the % of income that goes for child care is often higher than 10%. This sheet can help you decide on a financial subsidy.

Job Categ.	Total Fam. Income	Age of Chldrn	Type Care &Cost	Fed Tax Credit*	Actual Cost	% Family Income
e.g. Secretary	$15,000	2 yrs.	fam.day care: $40/week	$1,296	$3,384	22.6%
		5 yrs.	center $50/wk $4,680/yr.			

*Using formula described in Appendix D.

initiatives to stimulate the development of child care and parent support policies. While cooperation among all sectors of society is necessary to change child care in this country, it is in the best interest of each employer to understand how the problems of parents in their work force may affect the company's own goals. A carefully targeted program addressing the needs of working parents can increase productivity (and profits).

The range of options for supporting working parents is wide—from donating money or in-kind services to an existing child care program to the creation and management of a full child care service. The effectiveness of the choice is determined not by the amount of money spent, but rather by how well thought out and planned the response is to the parents' needs.

To get the most from dollars allocated to this issue, a company must find out (1) the needs of its work force, (2) its company's philosophy and goals as they relate to child care, and (3) what child care services already exist in the community. Worksheets 1, 2, and 3 will help you identify types of child care problems your employees may be having and the degree to which the entire work force is affected.

NOTES

1. U.S. Bureau of Labor Statistics, June 1985.

2. U.S. Department of Labor, Office of the Secretary, Women's Bureau, *20 Facts on Women Workers*.

3. U.S. Department of Labor, Bureau of Labor Statistics, March 1987.

4. A. Bernstein, "Business Starts Tailoring Itself to Suit Working Women," *Business Week*, p. 51.

5. Fact Sheet No. 85-4, U.S. Department of Labor.

6. U.S. Census Bureau, November 1986.

7. Report #86-345, U.S. Department of Labor, Bureau of Labor Statistics.

8. U.S. Census Bureau, November 1986.

9. Washington Business Group on Health, "Promoting Prenatal Health in the Workplace," p. 1.

10. U.S. Department of Labor, "Economic Responsibilities."

11. "Women Who Maintain Families," U.S. Department of Labor, Women's Bureau, Fact Sheet No. 86-2.

12. U.S. Census Bureau, November 1986.

13. AFL-CIO, "Child Care: Slow Progress, Pitiful Funding," p. 6.

14. U.S. Department of Labor, Fact Sheet No. 86-2.

15. Catalyst Career and Family Center, *Corporations and Two-Career Families*, p. 4; Louis Harris and Associates, Inc., *American Family Report, 1980-81*.

16. Chapman, "Executive Guilt," p. 35.

17. *Boston School-Age Child Care Coordination Project: A Progress Report*. School Age Child Care Project, Wellesley College Center for Research on Women. October 1987, p. 3.

18. U.S. Bureau of the Census, *After-School Care of School-Age Children: December 1984*, and U.S. Bureau of the Census, *Who's Minding the Kids?*

19. Collins, "Latchkey Children," p. C1; and *Boston School Age Child Care Coordination Project*, p. 3.

20. U.S. Bureau of the Census, *Who's Minding the Kids?*

21. Lydenberg, "Child Care Update."

22. Hofferth and Phillips, "Child Care in the United States, 1970 to 1995," p. 559.

23. Galinsky, "Investing in Quality Child Care," p. 11.

24. Long and Long, *The Handbook for Latchkey Children and Their Parents.*

25. Kamerman, *Parenting in an Unresponsive Society*, p. 2.

26. U.S. Bureau of the Census, *Who's Minding the Kids?*

27. New Jersey Division of Youth and Family Services, Research and Quality Assurance.

28. Chapman, "Executive Guilt," p. 35.

29. White House Conference on Families, "Work and Families," Report to Corporate Leaders, Washington, D.C., October 22, 1980.

2

CHILD CARE, CORPORATIONS, AND THE BOTTOM LINE

"Executive Guilt: Who's Taking Care of the Children,"[1] "Child Care: Your Baby?"[2] and "The Child Care Dilemma"[3] are just three of the many lead articles about child care to appear recently in the nation's most popular and prestigious magazines and newspapers. These articles urge business and government to begin responding to the needs of working parents.

Corporations with family-support policies in place are benefitting from press coverage of the issue. Representatives of these corporations, for example, Harry L. Freeman, executive vice president of American Express Company, are speaking out in favor of employer (and government) support for working parents. In a speech before the Select Committee on Children, Youth and Families of the U.S. House of Representatives on March 10, 1987, Mr. Freeman said,

American Express is involved [in child care] because the child care problems in America have reached crisis proportions. Corporations cannot ignore their responsibility...not if they want to attract and retain productive employees...not if they want to do business in economically healthy communities. The private sector must operate as a partner with the public sector to see to it that the quality and supply of child care meets the growing needs of our nation.[4]

According to the Conference Board, more than 3,000 employers offer some form of child care support. While this represents a small proportion of all employers in the United States, it has increased 30-fold since 1978. At that time, the National Employer-Supported Child Care Project identified 105 employer-supported child care programs.[5]

Research from Beaver College found that 75 percent of the employers responding reported that, much to everyone's surprise, they expanded rather than tightened their programs for working parents during recent difficult economic times. Their explanation: "Benefits far outweigh costs."[6]

A soon-to-be-published update by Sandra Burud of the National Employer-Supported Child Care Survey found a trend among employer support programs toward including more than one component, for example a child care center and a resource and referral program. In addition, child care support programs are being developed in all types of corporations throughout the country, not just in female-intensive industries.[7]

Still other research shows that many companies are unaware of the need for child care support and the options that can meet these needs. A study by the Massachusetts Industrial Financial Agency and the Policy/Action Institute of Transitional Employment Enterprises of 64 medium-size firms (median of 120 employees) found:

—Few firms know the child care needs of their workers.

—Companies hesitate to become involved in this issue because they do not see a need and because of liability and cost implications.

—Employers lack the expertise and organization necessary.

—Interest in joint child care efforts is equally high regardless of the proportion of women workers in the firms. However, firms with large proportions of women workers are more likely to be interested in company sponsored centers.

—Support from top management is necessary for child care consideration. In fact, the institute observed that "only when the issue was raised at the executive level was either additional study ordered or a child care center established."[8]

The impact on businesses of programs for working parents can be looked at under several headings: recruitment, turnover, and absenteeism of targeted groups of employees; public relations and corporate image; the nature of work; morale; employee' concerns and corporate awareness of these concerns; executive interest; and government incentives.

Data are becoming available that document the relationship between productivity and child care options. It is becoming clear that employer support for parents can make a difference in worker productivity and ultimately in the profit a company makes.

ENHANCING RECRUITMENT, DECREASING TURNOVER

Employees often represent a significant investment by a corporation. Recruiting and training new workers can cost an employer from several thousand dollars to well over $50,000 per employee. Additionally, it takes some time before the employee is functioning at the optimum level. Therefore, the loss of employees who have been with a company for a while can be costly.

Over the last ten years, the majority of new recruits into the work force have been women.[9] Many of these women are filling highly skilled positions in professions such as finance, law, and engineering. Among high-tech workers, turnover rates can be as high as 35 percent, and women are being hired at even greater rates.[10] At a Northeastern engineering firm, women hired as engineers jumped from 6 percent of all the engineers hired in 1977 to 17 percent just six years later.

Since many of these women have or will have children at some time during their work lives, employers with family-oriented policies report having an edge in recruiting these women. For example, William, Cutler and Pickering, a 144-partner law firm in downtown Washington D.C., uses an innovative child care program that provides emergency care for employees' children to attract attorneys.[11]

Hospitals are experiencing an acute nursing shortage.[12] A study conducted by the author found that in one Southern hospital several positions for critical care nurses had not been filled for more than a year.

The Greater New York Hospital Association, in a 1982 survey, found that child care, more than housing, parking or salaries, was central to the nursing shortage.[13] One reason is that nurses work shifts around the clock, on weekends and holidays, and often on a rotating or changing basis. These schedules do not conform to traditional child care hours. By the same token, a study by the National Association of Nurse Recruiters reported that day care is one of the most effective benefits for retaining nurses.[14]

In the early 1980s, the cost of recruiting one registered nurse, according to an administrator at Pioneers Hospital in Brawley, California, was $8,000. In 1981, hospitals in the Los Angeles area alone spent over $4 million to recruit nurses. Pioneers Hospital reduced its turnover rate to 4 percent, compared with the statewide rate of 48 percent, since the establishment of its child care center. Savings on recruitment and turnover add up to about $80,000 per year.

The Park View Hospital Child Care Center in Nashville, Tennessee, cost the hospital $50,000 per year compared with the former recruitment campaigns of $150,000 per year.[15]

Indeed, hospitals, more than other employers (except universities), have developed child care programs. Research by Judith D. Auerbach confirms that the number one reason that hospitals develop child care programs is to recruit and retain nurses.[16] One hospital she surveyed reported that before the development of their child care center, parent employees had a 40 percent turnover rate. In 1982, parent employees using the center had a 24 percent turnover rate, compared with 33 percent for the entire hospital. The hospital estimates a savings of $159,600 per year as a result of the program.[17]

Similarly, Control Data's 1973 study found that mothers using the Northside Child Development Center had a 25 percent lower turnover rate than mothers not using the center.[18]

Fel-Pro, a gasket company in Skokie, Illinois, has many innovative employee programs and policies, including a summer camp for 300 children and a day care center. The turnover rate of employees has gone down considerably since inception of these programs and is now negligible. The company receives 10 applications for each available job, at a time when entry-level jobs are difficult to fill.[19]

Table 3
Percent of Women Who Would Work
if Affordable Child Care Were Available, 1982

	Working	Would work
Married	46%	12%
Unmarried	59	17
Never Married	50	24
White	47	12
Black	56	23
High School Dropout	59	23
High School Graduate	48	14
College Educated	56	7
Family Income less than $15,000	45	20
$15,000-24,000	49	11
$25,0000+	53	6

Source: Martin O'Connell and David E. Bloom, *Juggling Jobs and Babies: America's Child Care Challenge.* The Population Reference Bureau, Inc., number 12, February 1987, 8.

A 1984 study found that on- or near-site centers

greatly reduced turnover rates among users.... For sixteen (94%) of the seventeen employers included in the analysis, the annual turnover rate for employees who used the child care service was lower, often substantially, than the annual rate for all employees. In 63% of the companies the rate of users was less than one half that of the whole company; in 53% of the companies, the turnover rate for users was zero.[20]

In fields with large concentrations of women, such as banking, child care is becoming an important recruitment tool. For example, one bank in Florida reported that after opening a child care center, 2,000 women applied for jobs, saying that they were home because they couldn't find child care.[21]

However, increasingly child care benefits are being offered to and used by men. Steelcase, in Grand Rapids, Michigan, has an extensive resource and referral and employee child care counseling service. It is staffed by two full-time and one part-time consultant. The employee population of 8,000 is only 20 percent female. In 1986, nearly half of the employees who used the service were male.

Experts on demographics report that employers will be facing a labor shortage through the year 2000 as the U.S. working-age population shrinks.[22] A 1982 study by the U.S. Census Bureau found that many more mothers would work—about 13 percent of those with preschoolers—if affordable child care were available to them. In particular, this is true of single mothers, black women who did not finish high school, and women from low-income families. Twenty-four percent more single mothers reported they would work if affordable child care were available to them (see Table 3).[23]

ABSENTEEISM

A study by the U.S. government found that nearly half a million working mothers lose time from their jobs because of problems with child care. The situation is more pronounced among women who use family day care—8 percent of the 1.3 million users lose time, while 1 percent of the 605,000 mothers using center care lose time from their jobs.[24]

Studies of employees in more than 33 corporations in Portland, Oregon, by Arthur Emlen and Paul Koren at Portland State University, found that parents of children in self-care, no matter what their economic status, were absent an average of 13 days a year. Other studies suggest that latchkey arrangements may actually be more common among higher income families, perhaps because parents perceive their neighborhoods as essentially safe for school-age children.[25]

Child Care Systems in Pennsylvania found that working parents lose, on average, 7 days a year because of child care problems.[26] Barbara Adolf and Karol Rose, in a study of a high-tech firm, found that 25 percent of the parent employees surveyed blamed child care-related problems for an average of 7 days away from the job per year.

In a *Fortune* study approximately two in five fathers and three in five mothers reported missing at least 1 workday during the past 3 months because of family obligations.[27]

Employers report that absenteeism rates have actually been lowered by implementing child care programs. Control Data reported a 22.5 percent reduction in absenteeism on the part of mothers using the center.[28] A hospital with a child care center reported a decrease in absenteeism from 5 percent to 1 percent compared to a 4 percent rate for all employees. Savings are estimated to be $90,000 per year.[29]

The Intermedics Child Care Center in Freeport, Texas, reported reduced absenteeism of several thousand hours by parents whose children were enrolled in the center. Combined with the reduction in turnover, a savings of approximately $80,000 per year was generated by the center.

One major cause of parent absenteeism is a child's illness. A study by the Learning Tree Day Care Centers in Minneapolis found that parents lost, on average, 5 days per year per child because of illness.[30] Kids' Klinic, a program for sick children operated by St. Luke Hospital in Fort Thomas, Kentucky, calculates that, since absent clerical employees cost their companies $100 per day and fees for the program are $16 per day, the program saved local businesses $110,000 in the first year of operation in providing care for some 728 admissions. The hospital also claims a $36,000 cost savings, based on revenue from the program ($11,000) and savings from their own employee absences.[31]

PRODUCTIVITY

In a survey by John Fernandez of employees of five high-tech companies (responses: 5,000 of 7,000 employees), 67 percent of parents reported that child care problems affected their productivity. About three-quarters of these parents had handled child care problems while at work. Nearly half of the mothers and one-quarter of the fathers reported spending unproductive time at work because of these problems.[32]

The Work and Family Life Study by Bank Street College found that one-third of the working parents at Merck, a large pharmaceutical company, "found it difficult or very difficult to manage their work and family life." Forty-one percent felt a "great deal of work/family interference, 38 percent experienced some interference, while 21 percent experienced none."[33]

Anxious people feel stress that can interfere with productivity. Managers speak of the "3 o'clock syndrome," when many working parents anxiously await news of their school-age children's safe return home. (The telephone company reports an increase in the number of phone calls at this time.) One manager of an automobile manufacturing firm said he learned through experience not to schedule any important work at 3 P.M. for his otherwise excellent secretary. He claimed she made more mistakes at that time than at any other time during the day.

When Honeywell surveyed its employees in 1980, it found that one of four working parents believed that stress caused by child care problems interfered with their productivity. Many of their problems had to do with finding reliable, quality care. As a result, Honeywell contributed funds as well as in-kind services to help establish an information and referral service, the Child Care Information Network, and remains a corporate subscriber to the service.

HEALTH CARE COSTS

A Bank Street College study conducted at two major corporations found a correlation between the breakdown of child care arrangements and parent illness. It found that "the instability of child care was...[a] more significant predictor of ill health for women with children under the age of 18 than most other aspects of their jobs. For men it was the second best predictor of ill health."[34]

Such ill health also costs a company money in increased medical claims and higher premiums. Researchers at Boston University found that more than one-third of working parents worry all or most of the time about their children, suggesting that eliminating or minimizing the problems that cause employees stress could have positive financial consequences.[35]

A strong argument for providing parents with information about prenatal care comes from the experience of Sunbeam Appliance Company in Coushatta, Louisiana. In 1984, about half of the health care costs of the company—$500,000—went toward the care of four premature babies born that year to employees. In 1985, one premature baby alone cost the company $250,000. Working with faculty members from Northwestern State University of Louisiana Nursing Education Center, the company developed a program that provides counseling and support through prenatal education classes and monitoring of pregnant employees throughout the term of pregnancy. The cost of the program is $15,000 per year. Since the program's inception, no employee has had a premature baby. Average costs per maternity decreased in 1986 by 90 percent from 1984 and by 83 percent from 1985, to $2,893. According to one report, "Sunbeam has gained in three ways: Improved health for employees and their families, enhanced employee relations, and greatly reduced medical expenses."[36]

PUBLIC RELATIONS AND CORPORATE IMAGE

Many corporations have found that by assisting working parents they enhance their image as institutions that care about people. The National Employer-Supported Child Care Project found that "85 percent [of the employers surveyed] reported that child care had a positive effect on public relations."[37]

The Corning Child Care Center in Corning, New York, is an example. The Corning Foundation, which funds educational and community-oriented programs, initiated the project and got community groups to participate. A film about the creation of the center, seen by audiences across the country, has spread the word that Corning is a company with up-to-date personnel practices.

Hill, Holiday, an advertising agency in Boston, has been featured on several television programs for its child care center, and was rated one of the top 40 U.S. companies in benefits by *Working Mother Magazine*. Fees for the center are on a sliding scale based on income, and the company subsidizes two-thirds of the operating budget.

IBM, American Express, and the Bureau of National Affairs are corporations that have initiated child care programs. Speakers from these companies, such as Jean Fraser and Dee Topal of American Express and Jean Lenahan of the Bureau of National Affairs, talk to business and community groups to promote corporate involvement in the needs of working families. Their activities help give their companies an innovative, humanistic image.

While it is hard to estimate the value of such publicity, in one study 9 companies estimated that their child care programs produce $13,000 in publicity each year.[38]

Increasingly, today's workers expect employers to respond to the needs of working parents.[39] Many corporations are finding it good business to meet these expectations. Of employers who are responding to the needs of working parents, 65 percent consider employer-supported child care successful in lowering turnover, 53 percent believe it is successful in lowering absenteeism, and 90 percent feel that it has raised morale.[40]

In the "comment" section of employee questionnaires developed by the author, time and time again respondents express thanks for being asked about their child care needs.

TYPE OF PRODUCT OR SERVICE

A company's product or service also affects its interest in child care. Companies that produce children's products, such as Stride Rite, which makes children's shoes, tend to consider child care programs as part of their corporate image. Companies specializing in health-related products also tend to support quality-of-life programs. Examples are Merck, in Rahway, New Jersey, and Hoffman-LaRoche, in Nutley, New Jersey, both of which are pharmaceutical companies.

FAMILY-OWNED BUSINESSES

Companies such as Geigco Brothers in Massachusetts (which manufactures men's clothing), Johnson Wax in Racine, Wisconsin, and Steelcase in Grand Rapids, Michigan (which manufactures office furniture), have developed child care programs for employees. Each is a family-owned, family-run business. Each is strongly committed to the family needs of its employees.

MORALE

Morale in a work force is hard to measure, but many personnel managers believe that morale affects productivity and that a good way to raise morale is through programs that respond to the needs of working parents. Recent studies bear this out.[41]

When the Official Airline Guides' Child Care Center was created in Oak Brook, Illinois in 1981, recruitment was not an immediate problem for the publishing company. Nevertheless, according to Susan Doctors, manager of personnel development, the president of Official Airline Guides gave the go-ahead for the center in the belief that "people want to work for a company that has progressive benefits." The company has not done a scientific study of how the center has impacted on recruitment, retention, and so forth, but a questionnaire filled out by new employees reveals that a number of them are favorably influenced by the presence of the center, even when they do not need or make use of it. Since its creation, women workers are returning to work sooner after giving birth than they used to. When a help wanted ad mentioned the center, the response was the best the company had ever received.

Steelcase developed an information and referral service and a family day care network. During the more than eight years that the program has been in place, the number of parents seeking the service has increased eightfold, from 62 parents in 1980-1981 (when 81 children were placed), to 167 parents (with 286 children placed) in 1983-1984, to 372 parents (with 533 children placed) in 1986-1987. Most of those using the service are two-parent families with both parents working. In 1986-1987, 46 percent of the parent-users were male employees.

Johnson Wax is another corporation that believes that supporting the family needs of employees raises morale and affects employee productivity. The company supports a child care center for employees' children.

When corporations change—through mergers, acquisitions, relocations, and so forth—many employees become anxious and uncertain about their future. Corporations that are sensitive to the family needs of employees during major personnel changes keep morale up. Along with its extensive relocation program (which pays moving expenses and part of an employees' house search, among other expenses) Diamond Shamrock Corporation in Dallas, Texas pays up to $100 for child care expenses incurred while employees are searching for a new home.[42]

EMPLOYEE CONCERNS AND
CORPORATE AWARENESS OF THESE CONCERNS

Employers learn about parenting problems from a variety of sources. Many companies have Employee Assistance Programs (EAPs) that provide counseling to employees about personal problems. It was through such a confidential service that Honeywell discovered that large numbers of parent employees were having problems related to child care. As a result of a follow-up survey, Honeywell hired a child care coordinator.

Many corporations have "round table" discussions or other forums for employee suggestions. At a large association, when child care was raised by several committee members, the director decided to commission a study of the issue.

Frequently, the employee relations manager is aware of child care concerns of employees and their impact on work. Other sources of information are career development managers, benefit managers, medical directors, and wellness instructors. Sensitive managers in all walks of corporate life may be aware of problems that employees are having and looking for ways to help these employees. Employees at all levels of corporations are beginning to talk about the stress they feel because of inadequate child care and other parenting problems. When a highly valued engineer told her superior that she was leaving her job because she could not find adequate child care for her infant, her boss broke all company precedents and offered her part-time work.

Sometimes groups of employees join together to express their needs to management. A group of women formed Concerned Women of La Roche and began to push for a child care center, which was opened in 1977. The Women's Network of the Bureau of National Affairs (BNA), a private firm based in Washington, D.C. that publishes information for business, prepared an extensive day care report in 1982. The report served as the impetus for BNA's donation of $5,000 to help start a child care resource and referral program for the D.C., northern Virginia, and Maryland area. BNA, as mentioned above, has since published reports on child care and supports its working parents in a variety of ways, including through information and referral, and a child care handbook.

In general, companies respond when employees express a need for help with child care responsibilities. At one hospital, an employee circulated a petition for child care, which resulted in the hospital's hiring Buck Consultants to study the issue. A survey by the Bureau of National Affairs found that, of 50 employers with child care assistance programs, 33 reported that they had initiated their programs either solely or in part because of employee requests.[43]

On the other hand, Auerbach found that although most employers take into account employee requests, their decisions are primarily based on a child care program's potential to enhance recruitment and retention of employees, and to lower absenteeism.[44]

EXECUTIVE INTEREST

Often a company responds to the child care needs of employees because an executive has a personal interest in the issue. The president of the Institute for Scientific Information (ISI) in Philadelphia, experienced firsthand the difficulty of finding adequate day care for his young children during the 1960s. In 1982, he opened a $1.5 million child care center for the children not only of ISI employees, but of other working parents in the community as well. The medical director of a large corporation, sensitive to the difficulty that two single parents in his department were having paying for child care, initiated a program to subsidize child care for employees.

Times are changing on all rungs of the corporate ladder. Even if a chief executive officer's wife stayed home with the kids, his daughter may well be a working parent. The president of a hotel chain initiated a program when his daughter, a teacher and a mother, urged him to help the working mothers in his employ. The result: the corporation created an on-site child care center.

Individuals at all levels of a corporation can be helpful and resourceful in exploring child care and parenting needs. In one case, the head of computer services volunteered his time to work on a child care study conducted by the author. The father of a seven-month-old child, and husband to a working woman, he felt a personal stake in the success of the study.

UNION INITIATIVES

During the last decade women comprised the majority of new entrants into the work force, and they are now heavily concentrated in white-collar and service-sector jobs.[45] Union membership among women has grown to 7 million members (14 percent of all women workers), or 41 percent of all union members.[46]

Unions have begun to take a leadership role in work/family issues. A 1984 survey by the AFL-CIO found that nearly two-fifths of nonunionized workers and almost half of all union members wanted help in finding child care.[47] In 1986, the AFL-CIO passed a resolution calling for policies that strengthen the family.[48] Even unions that primarily represent men, such as the United Mine Workers and United Steel Workers, have made work/family issues a priority in contract negotiations. For example, the United Auto Workers included child care resource and referral (R&R) in their 1987 settlement with the Ford Motor Company. The R&R will be "launched, coordinated and evaluated through the joint UAW-Ford National Development and Training Centers."[49]

Unions that have been particularly active in promoting child care support include those with a large female membership—the Amalgamated Clothing and Textile Workers, the International Ladies' Garment Workers, and the Newspaper Guild. Unions representing government workers, such as the American Federation of State, County and Municipal Employees and the California State Employees' Association, have also played a key role in developing child care and parenting initiatives.

GOVERNMENT INCENTIVES

Federal, state, and city governments encourage employers to support working parents in two ways: (1) by disseminating information about the costs/ benefits of employer support, and (2) by providing tax advantages for dependent care assistance plans or other types of child care support and penalties to corporations that do not treat pregnancy as they treat other disabilities.

Raising Awareness

The Women's Bureau of the U.S. Department of Labor promotes employer support for child care by sponsoring conferences for large- and medium-size corporations and small businesses, and disseminating information (books, a video, and so on) about program options. A number of states, cities, and counties have also hosted conferences with businesses to raise the consciousness of employers to the needs of working families.

The Department of Human Services of Tennessee established a team of consultants to assist employers in assessing the needs of their employees, and created a film to explain child care options and benefits to employers.[50] New Jersey has a corporate child care team appointed by the governor to stimulate interest in child care support and to publish data on programs that have been developed in the state.

Cities are also encouraging employer support for working parents. The mayor of Pittsburg hosted a breakfast meeting of CEOs and executive directors of local corporations to elicit their support for child care.

The federal government and several states including New York, Massachusetts, New Jersey, and Pennsylvania have developed child care centers for employees, to meet their employees' needs and serve as models to business.

Other innovations encourage employers to build on government initiatives. For example, Massachusetts, New Jersey, and Connecticut have funded the development of statewide resource and referral programs, and are encouraging employers to invest in these and other child care programs. New York provided seed money to nonprofit groups sponsoring after-school programs. The California Child Care Initiative and New York Neighborhood Child Care Initiative have included government funding in conjunction with corporate monies to expand family day care. A project of seminars and self-help groups developed by Buck Consultants for the New Jersey Division of Pensions is seen as a model for other state agencies and corporations.

Providing Tax Advantages

There are tax advantages to the employer for providing or supporting child care. Child care expenditures intended to benefit the employer in terms of reduced absenteeism and turnover are deductible as business expenses to employers that are profit making.

Employers can make contributions to tax-exempt child care programs, information and referral services, and so forth. In addition, companies can set up their own charitable foundations to fund child care programs.

The Economic Recovery Tax Act of 1981 established the Dependent Care Assistance Plan (DCAP), which provides a mechanism for employers to offer financial assistance for child care. This assistance is not taxable as income to the employee. (For more information, see Chapter 3.)

Such legislation is persuasive in stimulating broad-based corporate initiatives. Besides the federal government, several states have enacted dependent care assistance plans in which certain employer and employee contributions toward child care expenses can be tax exempt.

An important initiative, developed by Massachusetts in 1985, allocated $750,000 for low-interest loans to small industrial businesses and consortia to start child care centers.[51]

A bill to allow tax credits to employers who provide child care facilities at or near the worksite was introduced at the 1987–1988 Congress. Senator Dennis DeConcini of Arizona, one of the bill's sponsors, said, "Our public child care system can serve only 5 percent of the young children who need this care. We need a rapid response by private business to assist their employees, and the employers need greater incentives to increase the supply of available child care."[52]

Other Legislation and Mandated Benefits

The majority of states have been promoting employer support through anti-discrimination statutes, legislation to guarantee disability leaves to pregnant women (see Chapter 4), or some type of parental leave.

Cities, such as San Francisco and Concord, California, are beginning to enact legislation mandating employer support for child care. Concord, for example, requires a one-half of one percent fee on commercial developments over $40,000. The money is used to fund low-interest loans for child care programs, provide grants to train child care providers, and subsidize child care for low- and moderate-income working families.[53]

The past several sessions of Congress have seen legislation introduced that would require employers to grant employees a certain number of weeks of unpaid leave of absence at the birth, adoption, or serious illness of a child; continuation of benefits during the leave of absence; and a guarantee of the same or equivalent job upon return to work. This legislation is opposed by business organizations, such as the U.S. Chamber of Commerce, which claim that, for small businesses in particular, the costs would be prohibitive. Those promoting the bill cite the fact that the United States is the only industrialized country without such support for parents. (For a more complete description, see Chapter 4.)

Nevertheless, the federal government "has not recognized proper day care as a national priority."[54] While there are a half-million pension and profit-sharing plans in the United States, child care, as an employee benefit, trails far behind.

Worksheet 4
Management Perspective: Manpower Problems

This chart can help you determine if some personnel problems are related to the needs of working parents. The financial loss to the company can be measured against the cost of a program for parents.

_____Job Category_____.
Clerical RN LPN Technician Administ.

Number of employees

   Number of males

   Number of females

Absentee rate/year

Turnover rate/year

Cost of recruit and
train 1 employee/year

Number who are parents

Comments:

Worksheet 5

Management Perspective: What Other Employers Are Doing for Working Parents

---

Identify employers in your geographic area and in the same industry and describe their child care support programs.

A. <u>Nearby Employers</u> <u>#Empl's</u> <u>Type Support</u> <u>Cost/Year</u> <u>Success/Probls.</u>
(banks, factories,
govern. offices,
hospitals, etc.)

e.g. XYZ Computers   450   vouchers $50,000 Some parents
                                                      can't use – not
                                                      enought licensed
                                                      child care prog's

B. Employers in
   <u>Similar Field</u>

C. Other Sites
<u>of Your Company</u>

Welfare Reform

There is increasing recognition on the federal and state levels that many women could go off welfare if they had access to education and training, and affordable child care. Congress is considering a number of bills to tie child care with "workfare" programs.

A number of states pay either all or part of the day care expenses for children under six years old to enable their mothers to work. Illinois, Massachusetts, California, Michigan, Oklahoma, Arkansas, Ohio, and South Carolina are examples of states that provide this support. Massachusetts spent $28 million on day care, nearly half of its $57.5 million budget for the "Employment and Training Choice" (ET) program in 1987. Parents receive vouchers of up to $10 per day for child care and transportation. The entire ET program costs on average $4,500 per person per year, compared with $8,000 to keep someone on welfare.[55] Worksheet 4 can help you identify personnel problems that may be related to employees' child care needs. Worksheet 5 provides a frame of reference for your company. It will help you consider your options in terms of how other employers are dealing with parents' needs.

NOTES

1. Chapman, "Executive Guilt," pp. 30–37.

2. Dilks and Croft, "Child Care: Your Baby?" pp. 16–22.

3. Wallace, "The Child Care Dilemma," pp. 54–60.

4. Harry S. Freeman, American Express Corporation, "Child Care: The Role of the Corporation." Speech before the Select Committee on Children, Youth and Families, U.S. House of Representatives, March 10, 1987, p. 7.

5. Burud, Aschbacher, and McCroskey, *Employer-Supported Child Care*, p. 5.

6. Renee Magid, "A Business to Business Approach: Employer Involvement in Child Care," paper presented at the National Alliance of Business Conference, September 20–21, 1983, Philadelphia, PA.

7. Sandra Burud, SUMMA Associates, Pasadena, CA.

8. Child Care: Employer Involvement Potential Explored. *Spenser's Research Reports*, December 1986, 007.6–19.

9. U.S. Bureau of Labor Statistics, Washington, D.C., June 1985.

10. Rodgers and Rudman, Inc., *Child Care Options for High Technology Companies: A Decision-Making Guide*, Massachusetts High Technology Council, Inc., Boston, 1982, p. 2.

11. Jensen, "Perks," p. 30.

12. "U.S. Hospitals Facing Shortage of Nurses," *The Journal of Commerce*, January 30, 1987.

13. The Greater New York Hospital Association, "The Nursing Shortage," unpublished report, April 1982, p. 12.

14. Barbara Lovenheim, "A Need for Nurses," *Working Mother*, April 1982, p. 12.

15. Paul B. Brown, "Band-Aids by the Boxcar," *Forbes*, August 31, 1981.

16. Auerbach, *In the Business of Child Care*, p. 161.

17. Ibid., p. 180.

18. Northside Child Development Center, *1973 Annual Report*. Minneapolis, MN, 1973.

19. Anthony J. Rutigliano, "Some Would Call It Paternalism," *Management Review*, July 1986, p. 34.

20. Dawson, Mikel, Lorenz, and King, *An Experimental Study of the Effects of Employer-Sponsored Child Care Services on Selected Employee Behaviors*, p. vi.

21. Densford, "Make Room for Baby," p. 19.

22. Remarks of Thomas Espenshade, October 15, 1986, Employee Benefit Research Institute, *BNA Pension Reporter*, October 20, 1986, Vol. 13, p. 1826.

23. O'Connell and Bloom, *Juggling Jobs and Babies*, p. 8.

24. "A Hidden Cost," *American Demographics*, September 1987, p. 20.

25. Arthur Emlen, "Does Child Care Affect Employee Productivity?" *Business Link*, Summer 1986, p. 5.

26. Child Care Systems, Lansdale, Pennsylvania.

27. Chapman, "Executive Guilt," p. 35.

28. Northside Child Development Center, *1973 Annual Report*.

29. Auerbach, *In the Business of Child Care*, p. 181.

30. Ibid.

31. Therese Droste, "Kids Klinic Provides Option for Working Parents," *Hospitals*, October 20, 1987, p. 40.

32. Fernandez, *Child Care and Corporate Productivity*, p. 14.

33. Ellen Galinsky, Diane Hughes, and Marybeth Shinn, "Work and Family Life Study Pinpoints Sources of Stress for Corporate Workers," *Family Resource Coalition Report*, Vol. 5, No. 2, 1986, pp. 8–9.

34. Galinsky, "Investing in Quality Child Care," p. 2.

35. Burden and Googins, *Balancing Job and Homelife Study*, p. 7.

36. "Prenatal Program: Healthy Births and Bottom Lines," pp. 44–48.

37. Burud, Aschbacher, and McCroskey, *Employer-Supported Child Care*, p. 27.

38. Ibid., p. 24.

39. Chapman, "Executive Guilt," p. 36.

40. Burud, Aschbacher, and McCroskey, *Employer-Supported Child Care*, p. 27.

41. Ibid.

42. Bureau of National Affairs, *Work and Family*, p. 127.

43. Bureau of National Affairs, *Special Survey Report: Child Assistance Programs*, Washington, D.C.: Bureau of National Affairs, March 26, 1987, p. 2.

44. Auerbach, *In the Business of Child Care*, p. 160.

45. Bureau of National Affairs, *Work and Family*, p. 208.

46. Ibid.

47. Ibid., p. 210.

48. Cathy Trost, "More Family Issues Surface at Bargaining Tables as Women Show Increasing Interest in Unions," *Wall Street Journal*, December 2, 1986, p. 70.

49. United Auto Workers Union, "Child Care Resource and Referral," *UAW-Ford Report*, September 1987, p. 13.

50. Bureau of National Affairs, "Tennessee Sets Up a Day Care Consultation Team," *Fair Employment Practices*, October 30, 1987, p. 132.

51. Steven D. Lydenberg, "Child Care Update," p. 5.

52. "Day Care Tax Credit Bill Introduced in Congress," *Spencer's Research Reports*,

August 14, 1987, p. 7.

53. Lydenberg, "Child Care Update," p. 5.

54. Anna M. Rappaport, "New Ideas in Employee Benefit Planning," *Journal of Pension Planning and Compliance*, Vol. 13:1, Spring 1987, p. 49.

55. Day Care Information Service, "Welfare Reform, The Issue for 1987, Part II: Action in the States and Washington, D.C.," *Day Care Information Service Special Reports*, Vol. 16, No. 6, March 2, 1987, p. 1.

3

HOW EMPLOYERS SUPPORT WORKING PARENTS: PART I

Employers are addressing the needs of working parents in a variety of ways, which fall into five categories:

1. Adjusting work life—flextime, part-time work, job-sharing, home-based work, supervisor training, maternity/paternity or adoption leave, and sick days for child care;
2. Providing financial assistance—DCAPs, flexible benefits, vouchers, and program discounts;
3. Support for existing programs—in-kind services and charitable contributions;
4. Providing information to parents—individual advisement, workshops or seminars, and resource and referral (R&R); and
5. Development of new programs—child care centers, consortia, sick child care, family day care, and school-age care.

The following two chapters will discuss each of these options in detail, giving examples of employers that have selected various alternatives. It will discuss the pros and cons of different approaches. Worksheets have been included to help you think through each option in terms of your particular situation.

ADJUSTING WORK LIFE

The Work and Family Life Study, conducted by Bank Street College of Education, asked working parents at Merck, a pharmaceutical company, what single change in the workplace would most improve their work and family lives. Nearly one-third (the largest group) picked changes in their work schedules.[1]

In meetings with women who are vice presidents of financial institutions, the author found that their greatest concern was for time with their children. The sensitivity of their supervisors to their need for flexibility in scheduling—for example to work on weekends at home in exchange for time off during the week—made a difference in their commitment to the company. Those who felt supported by their supervisors put in even more time than they had to because they were so grateful for the help.

A number of companies have instituted programs that offer options in work schedules. Working parents may find these new schedules better suited to their child care needs. Some of the programs that have been especially helpful for working parents include flextime, job sharing/part-time work, maternity/paternity or adoption leave, and sick days for child care.

Flextime (Flexitime)

Flextime allows employees to have some leeway about starting and finishing times while working the normal number of hours. During certain "core hours," all employees must be at work. Nearly 3 out of 10 businesses use flextime, according to an Administrative Management Society study, up from 15 percent in 1977 and 22 percent in 1981.[2]

Dr. Halcy Bohen's study of 700 people on flextime indicated that most workers loved the program, but that its impact on family life proved hard to measure.[3] It seems that flexible schedules alone are not enough to resolve the conflicts between work and family responsibilities. Some benefits are apparent, however. Winnet found that people on flextime spend an additional 55 minutes per day with their families.[4]

In 1985, the American Management Association conducted a survey of white clerical workers in 300 firms and found that flextime improved productivity and morale. They found that nearly 25 percent of banks, 40 percent of insurance companies, and 20 percent of public utilities had flextime. Companies reported that the quality of work improved with flextime, while lateness and overtime decreased. Employees reported greater job satisfaction.[5]

A survey by the American Society for Personnel Administration showed that although the 5-day, 40-hour workweek is still the most common schedule, many new options are being adopted by companies. The survey of 456 organizations found that nearly half (45 percent) of the companies with flexible schedules were service organizations. Twenty-six percent were manufacturing companies. One positive result of flexible work schedules was improved employee job satisfaction.[6]

A May 1985 population report found that 13 percent of working women and 14 percent of working men were on flextime schedules.[7] The Bureau of National Affairs reports that advantages of flextime include, "increased productivity, since employees are happier with their schedules; and reduced sick leave and personal leave, since employees can more easily handle personal matters during the nonworking hours."[8] On the other hand, two disadvantages are: there might not be enough staffing during non-core hours, and communication and coordination of work among employees on different schedules is more difficult.

Variations of flextime include:

Flexitour—Employees may preselect their daily starting time and change to a new schedule at specified intervals.

Modified flexitour—Employees may modify their daily starting time without regard for intervals.

Gliding schedule—Within specified time periods, employees may vary their starting and departure times from day to day, e.g., 7:00–9:00 A.M. and 3:00–6:00 P.M.

Variable day—Employees may vary the length of the workday as long as they are present for a predetermined core period.

Variable week—Employees may vary the length of the day and the workweek as long as they are present for the core period and work at least the required number of hours biweekly.[9]

As a result of the Federal Employees Flexible and Compressed Work Schedules Act of 1978, employees of federal agencies have flexibility in arranging their schedules.

Other flexible work arrangements include flexibility during the work year—in terms of arranging the work load over the year—and compressed work schedules. In this case, employees work the equivalent of a full week in fewer than five days; that is, each workday is longer than eight hours. As of May 1985, 2.9 million full-time workers had compressed workweeks. The percent of full-time workers on compressed workweeks rose from 1.7 percent in 1972 to 3.9 percent in 1985.[10]

Part-Time Work

According to the U.S. Bureau of Labor Statistics, a job that takes less than 35 hours per week is part-time. Approximately 18.6 million U.S. citizens—about 17.5 percent of the work force—work part-time.[11] Women make up about three-quarters of the part-time work force, with the single largest group being married women. About 20 percent of all working women have part-time jobs.[12]

While part-time work enables women to spend more time with their families or gain new skills, drawbacks are that such work is often low paying and without fringe benefits.

Job Sharing

Job sharing refers to a situation in which two or more workers share one job. They may be split days, or alternate days or weeks. Less than 1 percent of the employee population is involved in job sharing.[13]

While this option may be preferred by employees with child care responsibilities, because it enables them to maintain their jobs and spend more time with their families, problems arise regarding benefits and seniority.

Job sharing is most popular among librarians, teachers, health care workers, and receptionists, according to the U.S. Bureau of Labor Statistics.[14]

Home-Based Work

Approximately 1.9 million employees perform traditional office jobs in their homes.[15] Two-thirds of these are women.[16] This option appeals to many employers because of the reduction in overhead and benefits required and the ability to recruit people who would not otherwise be available. However, employers do not like the lack of supervision over home-based employees.

About 300 companies nationwide offer home-based work, particularly for telecommunications and computer jobs.[17] Companies offering home-based work include Pacific Bell, J.C. Penney, Control Data, New York Telephone, Blue Cross and Blue Shield of South Carolina, and Shearson-American Express.

A major problem with home-based work is that employees have difficulty managing children while they are working. A City University of New York survey found that half of professional and clerical home-based workers with preschool children had to find child care in order to manage. In addition, a study by the Russell Sage Foundation reported that many employees of a Wisconsin insurance firm quit within two years of working at home because they could not manage taking care of their children and working at the same time.[18]

Temporary Work

One of the fastest growing trends in industry in the United States is temporary work. In 1985, 695,000 people were involved in temporary work; by 1995, the number is expected to jump to over 1 million.[19] Today, 1 in 13 new jobs is temporary.[20]

Some temporary help organizations provide employees with benefits. Many women prefer temporary work because of the flexibility it affords them. Employers may use temporary help to adjust the work force to correspond with changes in work load, to contain benefits costs, and to provide flexibility in the work force, among other reasons.

States and Alternative Work Schedules

Several states have developed innovative programs that give employees flexibility in meeting their family needs. For example, New York offers part-time work and job sharing with prorated benefits. A pilot project for managerial-level employees is the Voluntary Furlough Program, in which employees can reduce their hours by 5 to 30 percent. Their schedules are agreed upon jointly with supervisors so that manpower needs of the organization are met.[21]

Educating Supervisors to the Needs of Working Parents

The Work and Family Life Study conducted by Bank Street College found that supervisor sensitivity was second only to scheduling in improving working parents' family lives and productivity at work. The study found that poor relationships with supervisors adversely affected not only productivity but also the health of workers.[22] In general, managers were not aware of the problems that parents faced on a regular basis, even though 30 to 40 percent of the parents were feeling stress much of the time. Further, managers were more likely to know about men's problems than women's. Some employees even felt that supervisors were more concerned about men's problems.[23]

Programs to train supervisors in the problems and needs of working parents can be well worth the cost in the extent to which they increase morale and productivity of working parents.

Sick Care Policies

Traditional sick leave policies allow time off only when an employee is ill. Recognizing that parents legitimately need some time off to care for a sick child, companies are beginning to provide "family days" rather than "sick days" as part of the employee benefits package.

Maternity Leave

All industrialized societies provide statutory supports to working parents when a child is born.[24] However, the range of assistance offered by the United States is narrower than most. The 1978 Pregnancy Discrimination Act declared that women affected by pregnancy, childbirth, or related medical conditions are to be treated the same as other employees with a disability. In other words, employers cannot discriminate against pregnant workers. However, this provision does not specifically address the issue of maternity leave.

The importance of maternity leave and its effect on parents, children, and work have only recently been recognized by corporations in this country. A survey by the American Society of Personnel Administration of 357 firms found that 80 percent provide either partially or fully paid pregnancy leave. Employers of between 500 and 1,000 employees are most likely to provide full pay during pregnancy leave. Of the respondents, slightly more than one-fifth provide such a benefit. Characteristics of firms that provide partial pay are those with fewer than 500 employees (35.5 percent), those that are located in the South (nearly 40 percent), and manufacturers (nearly 36 percent).

In addition, length of service or eligibility for short-term disability determines the amount of pregnancy pay in slightly more than 14 percent of the respondents and in nearly one-quarter of the firms with over 1,000 to 2,500 employees. In only about 4 percent of the firms is pay determined by status— whether exempt, nonexempt, management, and so on.

More than one-third of the respondents reported that employees returning from pregnancy leave are guaranteed their former positions. Nearly 30 percent guarantee a comparable job at the same rate of pay.

Extended leave without pay is provided by 64.7 percent of the respondents. Only 2.2 percent provide paid child care leave. On average, employees remain at home between one and three months after childbirth.[25]

Another survey of more than 2,200 firms, done by the National Council of Jewish Women in 1987, found that 12 percent of firms offered 18 weeks of parental leave with job protection; slightly more than 25 percent offered medical leave with job protection; and about 40 percent offered medical benefits to employees on parental leave.[26]

A study by Catalyst in 1986 of Fortune 1,500 companies found that 95 percent provide short-term pregnancy disability leave for 5 to 8 weeks. Slightly more than one-half permitted unpaid leave with job guarantee beyond 8 weeks. Forty-six percent provided no parental leave to part-time employees. One-quarter offered a lower level of benefits to part-time workers.[27]

A study by the Congressional Research Service in 1985 found virtually no difference in maternity leaves between union and nonunion companies. One difference, however, appeared to be that nonunion companies tended to provide a pay benefit while union companies tended to stress job guarantee.[28]

The federal government is considering mandating unpaid parental leave. The Family and Medical Leave Act (HR 925, S 249) would require employers with more than a certain number of employees to provide employees with 10 weeks of unpaid leave on the birth or adoption of a child, and a job guarantee when they return. Since many women work for small companies that would be exempt from the law, a study by the National Commission on Working Women found that 77 percent of women in jobs that are nonprofessional or low paying could not afford to take such a leave. The Act requires that a panel explore paid leave, as well.[29]

States, on the other hand, are taking the lead in providing such benefits. Twenty-eight states were involved in legislation of this nature during the 1987 legislative session. At least 7 states guarantee disability leaves to pregnant women. Five guarantee leaves through antidiscrimination statutes.[30]

In 1987, 5 states enacted maternity or parental leave laws so that a total of 15 states have such laws. Sixteen other states are considering them.[31] There is some evidence that despite the laws, pregnancy discrimination exists. Unfortunately, many women cannot afford the fees necessary to take legal action.[32]

Paternity Leave

Bernard Hodes Advertising Agency found in a 1985 study that 1 in 7 companies surveyed had paternity leave policies.[33] Catalyst found that one-third of 384 employers surveyed offered unpaid paternity leave for 1 to 6 months, with job guarantee, similar to maternity leave. However, few fathers take these leaves. Rather, they typically take a few days off at the birth of a child, using vacation time or unpaid personal days. One reason may be that companies tend to frown on men taking paternity leave. The Catalyst study found that two-thirds of employers viewed such leave negatively.[34] However, one-quarter of the employers reported that they were favorable about men taking 6 weeks or less for paternity leave.

Adoption

Approximately 40 employers offer coverage of adoption costs as part of their employee benefit package.[35] Bank of America in San Francisco has been offering such a benefit since 1983. The employee pays the first $250 in covered expenses and the company pays up to $2,000 of the remainder. Employees who adopt foster children, step children, or children from overseas are eligible. Fees covered include agency fees, court costs, and legal fees, among others. From 1983 to 1985, 40 employees were reimbursed for adoption fees. All but one of the children were newborns.[36] Other employers that offer adoption benefits include IBM, Pitney Bowes, Pfizer, and Xerox.

Dealing With Workplace Reproductive Hazards

Today, women work well into their pregnancies. With the growth of technology, the need to protect pregnant women against dangers of chemicals, viruses, and other hazards on the job has increased. While the Occupational Safety and Health Administration (OSHA) mandates standards, many people believe these do not adequately cover the vast number of hazards that exist. Also, there is little awareness on the part of employers and employees of these problems.[37]

PROVIDING FINANCIAL ASSISTANCE

For many companies, providing employees with a direct financial benefit to help pay for child care is very appealing. Such a benefit can be funded by the employer only, by the employee only through salary reduction, or by both the employer and the employee. Monies given to the employee in this way are nontaxable. To provide a financial benefit of this nature, the company must set up a dependent care assistance plan.

Dependent Care Assistance Plans

The Economic Recovery Tax Act of 1981 (ERISA) established the Dependent Care Assistance Plan (DCAP). With a DCAP, employer assistance to employees for child care is not considered taxable income for an employee, even though it remains deductible by the employer. An employee can exclude from taxable income as much as $5,000 per year under a DCAP, resulting in great tax savings. DCAP programs commonly take one of three forms:

1. the employer can reimburse participating employees for their child care expenses;
2. the employer can make payments directly to providers of child care for children of employees;
3. the employer can establish a child care service (child care center, family day care, and so on) for children of employees.

Under the reimbursement of employees option, the employee pays the child care provider directly, and the employer reimburses the employee for qualifying expenses. Reimbursement payments may be funded in several ways: (1) the employer can pay some or all of the reimbursement; (2) reimbursement payments may be given in lieu of raises; or (3) the employee may elect (for tax purposes) to reduce his or her salary by the amount of qualifying dependent care payments up to $5,000 for a single individual or $2,500 for a married individual filing separately. (For example, an employee with a $25,000 salary and $5,000 in dependent care costs could reduce his or her salary to $20,000 and he or she would receive $5,000 in dependent care reimbursement payments in addition to the salary. This is known as "salary reduction.") An employee may not reduce his or her salary below the salary of the lower earning spouse. If the spouse is a student or disabled, the limit for the care of one child is $200 per month and for two children is $400 per month.

The salary reduction plan is usually preferred by employers, since the DCAP is thereby funded at no dollar cost to the employer. The employer saves the FICA and Federal Unemployment Tax Act (FUTA) taxes on the employee's salary and only has to pay for the design and administration of the plan. For small employers, the administration is relatively simple.

One problem with a salary reduction plan is the "use it or lose it" provision. Employees must decide in advance of each plan year exactly how much to allocate (up to the $5,000 limit) to the dependent care account. Any monies they do not use will be forfeited. (Also, the monies are given as they accumulate in the account; they are not advanced to the employee.)

A DCAP can be established as part of a cafeteria benefit plan (flexible benefit plan), or it can be established as a stand-alone benefit—as a flexible spending account. Most large corporations that set up flexible spending accounts include a medical reimbursement option as well. Since this makes the benefit applicable to all employees, no one has reason to resent the "special treatment" of working parents.

As a result of the Tax Reform Act of 1986, employers must meet the discrimination tests of Section 89 of the Internal Revenue Code in order to retain the tax advantage. The discrimination tests are intended to make sure that more highly paid employees do not receive benefits that are of much greater value than those of lower-paid employees. The specific discrimination tests that must be applied are determined by the type of plan that is established.

There is some discrepancy about how many employees are covered by dependent care assistance plans. A U.S. government study reported that in 1985, 200,000 employees were included in dependent care assistance plans, representing 1 percent of all employees.[38] According to the Conference Board, in 1987 at least 1,500 employers (many of them large) had flexible benefits with the dependent care option. This suggests that the government figure is low. Buck Consultants estimates that approximately 15 percent of large employers offer some form of dependent care reimbursement, and the number is growing.

The actual utilization rate of DCAPs funded by salary reduction for most companies is around 5 percent of the employee population. To put this in perspective, less than 40 percent of a typical employee population are parents, and only 20 percent of these have children under six. However, it is true that among those eligible for the financial assistance, the utilization rate is low. One problem is that much child care is informal and providers do not want to report their income. However, as providers become professionalized, they may be more willing to become "visible." The "use it or lose it" provision may inhibit some employees from signing up for the salary reduction benefit. In addition, the benefit is complicated and must be explained, so poor communication can drastically reduce utilization.

Community Service Society is an advocacy organization that employs about 400 in New York City. The Society instituted a dependent care benefit in 1984 which is funded solely by the organization. Employees are reimbursed up to $400 for child care expenses. Bettina Seidman, Director of Human Resources, says that although it may not seem like a lot, many employees, particularly single mothers, appreciate it. About 12 percent of employees utilize it.

Some companies offer financial support for special situations. For example, Hewitt, an employee benefit consulting firm, reimburses employees for baby sitting expenses incurred because of travel for work.

Such benefits may be limited to employees earning below a certain amount or whose children are under a certain age. Polaroid Corporation offers financial assistance to employees based on family income.[39] Measurex Corporation offers employees $100 per month toward the care of infants up to one year old. Zayre reimburses employees up to $20 per week for their children under five years old.

The Ford Foundation established a Child Care Assistance Policy in 1972. At that time, the foundation covered 50 percent of the typical weekly rate for child care paid by employees, with small additional amounts for those using licensed care because it is usually more expensive. In 1979, the reimbursement rate was changed to match the rates set by local and federal agencies. The Ford Foundation offers assistance to full-time employees with gross family incomes of $25,000 or less. (The original maximum of $20,000 was increased in 1980.)

Income restrictions on eligibility help keep the overall costs down, but they also prevent most of the professional staff from participating in the program. The number of participants in the Ford Foundation program has never exceeded 28 (or 10 percent of the eligible nonexempt employees). In 1983, the total cost of the program for all users was $10,505. This provided each parent with an average of $875 per year for child care expenses.

One innovative program was developed by Klein-Kaufman Corporation which operates 13 MacDonalds stores on Long Island. Of 800 employees, 40 are working mothers. Jonas Kaufman found that these employees were among the company's best workers. In fact, 10 percent of managers were working mothers, many of whom had started at minimum wage level.

Since child care was a serious problem for many, Kaufman and Klein developed an innovative child care reimbursement plan, the Babysitter Assistance Program. After some experimentation, the plan was based on the number of hours worked. Employees who work a minimum of 25 hours a week receive $50 toward their child care. Those working between 20 and 24 hours a week receive $40 toward care, and those working between 15 and 19 hours a week receive $30 toward their child care.

Flexible Benefits

A national study conducted by Buck Consultants in 1986 found that nearly three-quarters of employees would change their benefits if they could and 70 percent would be willing to pay to have greater choice in their benefits.

Flexible benefit plans allow employees a degree of choice. Depending on the plan design, employees may choose among different levels of a particular type of benefit (such as medical plans) or among different benefits. Typically, a "menu" might include various combinations of health benefits, life insurance, long-term disability, vacation, dental, dependent care, cash, group legal, and savings plans (40 lk). Some employees may choose dependent care rather than cash or group legal benefits.

Employers can design the benefit options with cost containment in mind. Duplication of benefits can be avoided. Less costly and less popular benefits can be "priced" to encourage employees to use them; however, important "core" benefits (such as medical) can be mandated to assure certain minimal levels of coverage.

Employee satisfaction is a major impetus for instituting flexible benefit plans. American Can found that five years after instituting flexible benefits, employee satisfaction with their benefits was 50 percent higher than that of employees nationwide. Ninety percent of American Can employees reported that they liked selecting their benefits each year.

Research shows that women, even more than men, prefer having a choice over their benefits. A study commissioned by the Employer's Council on Flexible Compensation found that 91 percent of the women and 80 percent of the men with flexible benefit plans prefer the "flex" plan to benefit plans with fewer choices. Seventy percent of the women and 19 percent of the men reported that flexible benefit plans allowed them to get benefits that other employers do not offer.

Fifty-six percent of the women said if they were looking for a job they would be more favorably impressed by an employer with flexible benefits than one without, compared with 26 percent of the men.[40]

According to John Haslinger, director of Flexible Benefit Consulting Services for Buck Consultants (an employee-benefit consulting firm), between 22 and 25 percent of mid- to large-size employers have instituted flexible benefit plans. About three-quarters of these plans are flexible spending accounts. The rest are more sophisticated flexible benefit plans. Haslinger sees growing interest on the part of employers in the more comprehensive flexible benefit plans, even with the current "uncertain legislative climate." (Congress is considering taxing benefits.)

Volvo North America Corporation, Rockleigh, New Jersey

Volvo's flexible benefit plan embraces some 1,500 employees throughout the country. With a population that is approximately 60 percent male and 40 percent female, Volvo employees work in a range of occupations—sales, service, importing, and manufacturing. The plan was designed to meet the diverse needs of employees and to provide the company with better control in managing and monitoring their benefits. As Keld Alstrup, director of Compensation and Benefits put it, "While we didn't need to cut costs, we felt we would be better able to manage our benefits in the future."

Volvo Options was designed with two essential criteria in mind: (1) so that no employee would be at risk by not having enough coverage in health, life, disability, and so on, and (2) so that the plan—design, communications, and administration—would be of the highest quality, to reflect the company's image.

The sophisticated program is based on a "Core Plus Option" involving medical, health care reimbursement account, dental, life insurance, dependent life insurance, accidental death and dismemberment (AD&D), business travel accident, dependent care reimbursement account, salary continuance, short-term disability, long-term disability, vacation and holidays, pension plan, 401k plan, and additional taxable cash income. In each area the program provides a core of benefits ensuring protection against catastrophic occurrences, and a range of options enables the employee to fine-tune his or her benefits as desired.

The Volvo Options program consists of four basic components:

1. A core of benefits in each major benefit area providing employees with protection against catastrophic occurrences;
2. A range of benefit options in each benefit area enabling employees to add to the core coverage in order to individually tailor their total benefit program;
3. A flexible credit formula that is the difference between the cost of the preflex program and the new core benefits; and
4. Flexible spending accounts that can be used to pay qualified dependent care expenses and qualified medical expenses. These accounts can be funded with employee authorized pretax salary reductions and/or employee flexible credits.

Implementation took less than five months to complete. In October and November, group meetings were held to explain the program to employees.

Brochures were distributed in "progressive disclosure," so that employees were not overwhelmed with all the information at once. A slide and audio presentation was developed along with worksheets to allow employees to play out their options. The plan opened for enrollment on January 1, 1987.

According to John Haslinger, consultant to the project, "Exactly 50 percent of those enrolled for the dependent care benefit are men and 50 percent are women, showing that child care is not a 'women's issue' but a 'family issue.' "

While at first, some people were suspicious about the flex program, now the program gets "only good feedback," says Keld Alstrup. In fact, research shows a 98.5 percent satisfaction level among employees. Says Alstrup, "That's good enough for me!"

Vouchers

Corporations can provide employees with vouchers to pay for a portion of their child care. The employer sets up an account with licensed providers that employees choose, or with an intermediary organization which then issues vouchers to qualifying employees. In the latter case, employees chose from programs that are part of the voucher system and the employer pays a fee to the agent for the service. One drawback is that not all child care programs used by employees necessarily participate in the system. In some cases providers may be required to pay a fee to the voucher organization. Since child care fees are generally low to begin with, child care providers may be reluctant to pay fees to the voucher organization, particularly if the child care programs are in great demand and have long waiting lists.

The Voucher Corporation

Based in Europe, this company originally provided vouchers to employers for food services. It expanded to child care in the United States in 1984. The employer pays a start-up fee of \$200 to \$900 and 3 to 7 percent of the total voucher amount. Communications materials are extra. The amount of money the employee chooses to deduct from his or her paycheck is sent by the employer to the Voucher Corporation, which then issues child care vouchers to the employee. The employee pays the provider with the vouchers. The provider then redeems the vouchers for cash from the Voucher Corporation.

Participating employers are given a list of programs that subscribe to the system, as well as reports about usage.

The employer saves on FICA and FUTA taxes. Providers pay one-half of one percent of the vouchers they receive in order to be part of the network. The Voucher Corporation takes care of all the paper work and administration. As in a flexible spending account, the benefit is funded by salary reduction.

One problem with the program is that providers who redeem vouchers must report their income to the Internal Revenue Service. Since 50 to 70 percent of providers do not report their child care earnings, many choose not to enroll in the program.[41]

Corporations subscribing to the system include Abt Associates Inc., Computervision Corporation, and Southshore Hospital in Massachusetts, among others. First Wisconsin National Bank contracted with the Voucher Corporation for employees at its Milwaukee headquarters in March 1986. Of 3,500 employees, 100 participate. The bank pays 4 percent of the total amount each month, but saves on taxes.[42]

For corporations that do not want to combine a dependent care benefit with a medical spending account this can be a good option. However, they should be sure that the child care programs the employees actually use are, or plan to be, part of the system.

4Cs of Central Florida

Community Coordinated Child Care (4Cs) administers a resource and referral service for three counties in Central Florida. Its data bank includes nearly 400 programs—child care centers, family day care homes and Head Start Centers, and YMCA Fun Clubs. Funded by local United Way agencies and county, state, and local governments, the agency also administers child care for low-income families. A handsome guide, funded by local business, provides information about selecting care and a list and photographs of child care programs in the area.

Under the Child Care Assurance Plan, 4Cs provides resource and referral services (help finding child care, counseling, and so forth) to employees of participating companies, and direct payments to employees' child care providers. The company pays an initial fee of \$500 and a percentage of employee child care fees (the employer decides in advance), with the remainder paid by each employee. Employers also pay a fee to 4Cs for administration. The higher the percentage of child care covered, the lower the administration fee. Employers receive monthly reports of usage. Overall, the cost comes to about $100 per child.[43]

Southland Corporation contracted with 4Cs for a one-year trial period. Southland pays 25 percent of employee's child care costs, up to $60 per week for infants and $50 per week for older children.

Polaroid Corporation, Cambridge, Massachusetts

Polaroid employs 13,000 in plants throughout eastern Massachusetts and in seven other states. Instituted in 1971, the voucher program provides a child care subsidy to employees on a sliding scale based on income and child care costs. Employees qualify whose family income is under $30,000. While employees choose their providers, these must be licensed. Polaroid pays the providers directly on a quarterly basis. Approximately 100 people use the subsidy each year.[44]

Program Discounts

Companies can arrange for employee discounts in local child care programs in much the same way they have negotiated reduced rates for employees for car rentals, hotels, and sports events. It is estimated that 300 employers currently contract with child care programs, usually for-profit chains. In most cases, the child care program offers a 10 percent discount to the employee, and in about one-half of the contracts, the employer contributes 10 percent of the fees so that employees get a 20 percent reduction in cost.

To be most useful, the programs selected by the employer must be convenient and appropriate to the needs of most of the employees with children.

Child Care Tax Credit

Employees can also qualify for a federal tax credit for child care. The credit is figured on a sliding scale, based on adjusted gross income. In a two-parent family, the amount of expenses eligible for the credit is limited to the amount of the lower of the two salaries.

For families with adjusted gross incomes of $10,000 and under, 30 percent of child care costs can be taken as a tax credit. The maximum amount eligible for the credit for one child is $2,400 and for two or more children is $4,800. For families earning more than $10,000, the credit is reduced by 1 percent for every additional $2,000 or fraction thereof of adjusted gross income. At incomes of $28,000 and above, the credit stays at a maximum of 20 percent of the amount the family pays for child care. (See Appendix D for the Tax Credit table.)

Legislation may be changing the amount of the tax credit and eliminating it entirely for parents whose incomes are above a certain amount.

Parents may claim the tax credit and/or any child care benefit they receive from their employers. If the employer benefit is funded by salary reduction, employees should calculate how much of the benefit to use (up to the $5,000 maximum) and how much of the tax credit to use. In practice, employees earning over $28,000 profit most from the employer benefit, whereas those below this figure should calculate the tax credit first.

States may also provide child care tax credits in addition to the federal credit. The New York State credit, for example, is generally equal to 20 percent of the federal credit.

SUPPORT FOR EXISTING PROGRAMS

There may be child care services already available either near your site or where parent-employees live. However, many existing programs are not sensitive to the needs of working parents. Frequently the hours are not ideal, children below a certain age (often infants) are excluded, and so forth. To make such programs more responsive to the employees' needs, a company may wish to donate in-kind services (products or resources) to them. A company can support existing programs through charitable contributions, or can purchase slots in a program for employees' children.

In-Kind Services

Companies have many resources from which child care programs can benefit. These include expertise in law, accounting, public relations, and other relevant fields. Many companies choose to support a particular program that serves their employees by donating such in-kind services. Not only does this save the child care program money, but the level of expertise offered by the company is usually higher than what the program could afford by itself.

Charitable Contributions

A corporation may make a charitable contribution of up to 10 percent of its taxable income to a nonprofit child care program. Many corporations have set up foundations to which they donate funds for educational, health, and cultural programs. Such foundations can create and fund nonprofit child care programs. The Corning Glass Foundation provided a grant to start the Corning Children's Center. It also provides a subsidy for the center's operation. Stride Rite funds its child care center through the Stride Rite Foundation. Under Section 501 (C)(3) of the federal tax code, an employer may establish a tax exempt child care center and make contributions to it. However, the center must be open to community children. The center can also obtain government subsidies if children from families who qualify for such funding are enrolled. For more information about how families qualify, check with your local welfare agency or Department of Social Services.

Company charitable foundations can fund a variety of child care programs. As mentioned earlier, BankAmerica and American Express, along with other corporations, have funded major initiatives in California and New York that recruit and train family day care providers.The Levi Strauss and Ford Foundations funded a demonstration project for school-age children. Use Worksheet 6 to identify child care related programs that your company already supports. Worksheet 7 can help you record parent usage of existing programs.

PROVIDING INFORMATION TO PARENTS

Providing information to parents is one of the simplest, least expensive forms of support an employer can offer employees. The method used to provide the information can be simply a written brochure or pamphlet, or the information can be given in face-to-face contact with an expert in the field of child care for working parents. The advantages of personal contact are obvious. The questions and concerns of working parents change as their children grow and develop. Three ways of providing information on a personal basis are individual advisement, workshops or seminars, and resource and referral.

Individual Advisement

When working parents have the opportunity to meet with a child care professional to discuss parenting concerns, they often find considerable relief from anxiety and guilt. Typically, the issues that parents raise in such meetings have to do with how to get quality care for their children, how to hire an appropriate caregiver, and how to improve the interaction between caregiver and child. Parents who work long hours or travel a lot may ask how to maintain close ties with their children while they are away.

A consultant can schedule half-hour sessions with individual parents throughout the workday. At the end of the day, the consultant can summarize the requests, helping management understand employees' needs.

Parents attend these sessions for a variety of reasons. They may prefer the privacy of the session, or their schedules may be suited to such consultations. Our experience is that executives seem especially interested in these sessions.

Phone consultation can also help parents cope with emergencies that arise or general concerns they may have. It is advisable, however, for the consultant to meet first with employees face to face to establish rapport and trust.

Workshops or Seminars

Workshops or seminars are an attractive option to many employers for several reasons. First, they are an inexpensive way to show parents that the company is concerned about their problems. Second, they can serve as an informal means of assessing the needs of parents. Third, they can be tailored to the specific needs and interests of the employee population. Finally, they can form the basis of a support group among parents.

Workshops and seminars allow participants to share ideas and experiences, and may include "hands-on" activities such as brainstorming, role playing, or problem solving. Although the large group sessions can be helpful and enjoyable to participants, especially when presented by a charismatic speaker, they rarely provide the intensity of individual learning or the support and satisfaction that the small-group workshop or seminar can provide. When groups are limited to fewer than 25 participants, "hands-on" activities and discussion can actually help employees solve their individual problems. For example, at a seminar at CBS conducted by the author, one woman manager talked about her two-year-old's feelings about moving to a new home and the loss of a much-loved caregiver. After a discussion about how to prepare the child for the separation, another mother in the group politely asked if she could have the name of the caregiver, as she was looking for someone to care for her child.

Participants report that one of the most satisfying aspects of the small-group seminar or workshop is the reassuring realization that other people have similar problems (guilt, for example), and that they are not alone. Since today's working parents often do not have time to talk with other working parents—either in their homes or on the park bench—to share observations, pleasures, and concerns about their children, the workshop or seminar can mean a lot.

Topics

Workshops and seminars can provide information about a wide range of topics of concern to working parents or employees planning to become parents—how to balance work and parenting successfully, how to locate and monitor care, what normal child development is, and so on. They can be scheduled as individual sessions or as a series. If planned as an individual session, the workshop usually covers a broad range of topics and tries to provide a little for a lot of employees. The author's experience with such sessions is that they are less satisfying for employees because, by necessity, they cannot deal with any topic in depth.

On the other hand, a session targeted to a specific audience and limited to one topic can be very successful. Typically, the employer identifies the main concern of employees, for example, "What is quality child care?" and makes it clear that this is what will be presented. Employees can be asked about their interest in other topics and, based on the response, future sessions can be planned.

Some employers choose to offer a series of sessions to meet the needs of a particular employee group. For example, the author designed a series of four seminars for new and expectant parents at American Express. The series was called, "Parenting in the '80s" and included an overview session; "Parenting in the '80s: What Works and What Doesn't," and three in-depth sessions: "Getting Ready for Parenting and Working," "Choosing Child Care and Making It Work," and "Take the Sting Out of Parental Guilt."

Another series conducted by the author was designed for employees of a state agency. In this case, a questionnaire was distributed to employees to find out their particular interests. Based on the returns, three parent groups were formed: (1) parents of infants, toddlers, and preschoolers; (2) parents of school-age children; and (3) single parents. The initial round of sessions provided comprehensive information relevant to each group. The specificity fostered a warm group feeling, which was one of the goals of the employer. Group leaders were trained by the author to conduct ongoing sessions and given technical assistance when questions arose.

Planning and Logistics

Sessions are typically held for one to one and one-half hours during lunch so that parents do not have to stay late and take time away from their children. Community Service Society, a nonprofit organization that provides support for the poor of New York City, scheduled workshops during lunch and into the afternoon worktime, showing employees that the sessions were highly valued.

Many employers provide a comfortable space and refreshments for the sessions to encourage a relaxed, informal atmosphere and to show that they want employees to attend. Such generosities add to the atmosphere of warm hospitality and make employees feel cared about.

Depending on the "corporate culture" and point of view of the employer, management from the personnel or benefit department may or may not attend. If the session is designed for a small group, some employers believe that management's presence inhibits employees, keeping them from sharing and solving their problems and accomplishing the goals of the session. Others believe that management presence is viewed as support. Management representatives can answer questions that may arise about benefits or company personnel policies that the workshop leader (who is usually an outside consultant) cannot answer. There are pros and cons to each approach, and a decision must be based on the goals and experience of each employer. In either case, however, confidentiality must be maintained.

If your company has a structure for offering information to employees, you can begin there. For example, many companies already offer sessions on "wellness" topics such as stress management, smoking cessation, safety, and so on. These may be under the auspices of the medical department, employee assistance program (EAP), employee relations and personnel, employee benefits, or community relations. In some cases, sessions are sponsored jointly by two or more departments, lowering the costs and gaining visibility for each, and providing each with an opportunity to introduce other services.

Selection of a Workshop/Seminar Leader

To find a consultant to lead workshops, ask people who have experience in the field. Contact employer-supported child care companies, local colleges, community resource and referral agencies (see next section), women's groups, and other employers. Talk with candidates, check their credentials, and try to observe them conducting sessions. (This may not always be possible because of confidentiality.) Discuss your requirement with the candidates and ask what they can do to implement your goals. Familiarize them with relevant personnel policies, such as maternity/paternity benefits, sick days, and so on. Be sure to advise them of any problems you anticipate, for example, questions about a new personnel policy. You would not want a leader to insist that mothers should not return to work until their babies are at least a year old if maternity benefits at your firm cease after four months.

Worksheet 8 can help you plan workshops for your employees.

Publicity

Workshops should be publicized one month in advance using regular in-house methods, whether bulletin boards, newsletters, or interoffice memos—preferably all. (See Sample Workshop Notice and Sign-up Form.) Often employees like to help with the communications—whether or not they are part of the art department—and will design attractive and catchy posters and logos for the occasion.

Procedures for signing up in advance, say two weeks, may include returning a sign-up sheet or making a telephone reservation by a certain date. This is helpful in three ways: you can anticipate how many people will be attending and arrange an appropriate room. You can remind people a few days in advance that the event is coming up. Finally, you can also have participants answer a few short questions, such as what the ages of their children are or what they would like to discuss at the session. The information obtained can help you tailor the session to the specific employees.

Fees

Most employers regard workshops and seminars as an employee benefit that is part of the cost of doing business. Most do not charge employees a fee for the sessions. Those who do charge a nominal fee, such as $5, believing that this makes the service more valued by employees.

Evaluation

It is helpful for seminar planners to get feedback from participants about the sessions. It also enables participants to share ideas and thoughts that they might not be comfortable discussing in the group.

An evaluation form can include a series of short open-ended questions, such as: "What did you like most about this session?" "What did you like least?" "What other information would you have liked included in the session?" and "What are your suggestions for future sessions?"

Participants can be asked to rate the session on a numerical basis. For example, on a scale from 1 to 5, "1" could mean "least helpful" and 5 could mean "most helpful," with the numbers in between representing increasing degrees of "helpfulness." See Worksheet 9 for examples.

Who Is Offering Workshops?

Many employers offer working parent workshops or seminars to their employees. Included are American Express, Time Inc., New Jersey Division of Pensions, Consumer's Union, Proctor and Gamble, Ciba Geigy, and PSFS Bank in Philadelphia.

Organizations throughout the country that provide consultants to conduct seminars include Buck Consultants, Bank Street College of Education, Parents At the Workplace, and Resources for Parents At Work, among others.

Resource and Referral

One of the most difficult problems for parents, particularly those who do not have relatives living nearby, is finding child care. Most programs are not listed in the telephone book. Even if they are, parents do not know where and how to begin choosing. With fears about child abuse, parents are especially skeptical about using providers whom they don't know.

Resource and referral agencies, which are usually community-based, private, nonprofit organizations, have been developed or expanded during the last several years to help parents identify child care in their communities. These agencies gather information from parents about their needs and preferences—ages of their children, type of care they want, what they can afford to pay, type of program they prefer, and so on. The agencies then provide parents with referrals, including at least two programs for parents to consider. Frequently, the service is provided over the telephone, with follow-up by mail.

Overall, there are nearly 600 referral agencies throughout the country.[45] A study by the Conference Board in New York City found that at least 500 corporations offer resource and referral to their employees. This represents a 60 percent increase since June 1985.[46]

Resource and referral agencies vary considerably in the information they provide. Some offer simple lists of programs with infrequent updates, while others have sophisticated computerized systems that track programs and their use. A few offer "vacancy control"—information about openings in programs. Vacancy control helps avoid the frustration parents feel when they call the referrals and find that there are no openings.

In 1984, IBM funded the creation of a nationwide resource and referral network for their 240,000 employees. Operated by Work/Family Directions in Boston, the network was the first of its kind to connect resource and referral agencies throughout the country. IBM donated personal computers to member agencies and provided training to help them develop the service.

How Corporations Can Be Involved

A company can buy into an existing resource and referral agency or develop its own in-house service. The choice depends on company goals, parent needs, and community resources. At minimum, the service may involve no more than membership in a computerized system or a direct telephone linkup with community programs.

Most resource and referral agencies provide the service to parents either free of charge or at a nominal fee. Corporations can contract with a resource and referral, paying a fee on a per capita basis (based on the number of employees in the corporation) or on a per case basis. On a per capita basis, fees range from $2 to $10 per employee, with the higher figure based on expectations of higher employee usage. On a per case basis, fees run from $60 to $100 per family per year. When a company contracts with a resource and referral agency, parents usually receive a more in-depth service than they would if they approached the agency as individuals.

Employers need to contract with resource and referral agencies in employees' home communities. Again, agencies vary considerably in the type of information they offer and the frequency with which they update their information. Resource and referral can be cost-effective in that it saves employees time and energy, reduces their stress and anxiety, and is tax deductible as a business expense or charitable contribution. Such a service combines easily with other types of support for working parents. Resource and referral can fit into a company's existing employee assistance program or its benefit or human resources department. Ideally, through a resource and referral service a company can respond to immediate needs while collecting data (needs assessment) on which to base decisions about additional support.

Some resource and referral contracts also provide employers with workshops for employees. Check to see what is offered, who will conduct them, and so on. Also, some agencies offer parents counseling on quality child care and advice on which kinds of programs are appropriate for different aged children, the pros and cons of the various child care options, how to interview caregivers, and so forth. Use Worksheet 10 to compare services offered by child care resource and referral agencies.

Expanding Child Care

By keeping track of requests for child care that are unmet, resource and referral agencies are in a position to identify areas of need and help expand the child care provider system. A portion of the funding from IBM enabled Work/ Family Directions to develop new child care programs, where a need was identified. The program saw a vast expansion of family day care and center care. Other large, nationwide corporations that have contracted with Work/ Family Directions for their employees include Kraft, McDonald, Mitre, Pepsico, Tandem Computers, and Xerox, among others.

Child Care Systems, a company based in Lansdale, Pennsylvania, provides employers with resource and referral on a nationwide basis. Clients include Allstate, Time Inc., Continental Insurance, and the Internal Revenue Service. Child Care Systems also solicits new providers where a need is evident, for example, in after-school care.

An innovative program was initiated by the BankAmerica Foundation in San Francisco. Along with other corporations and the state, it provided $700,000 in start-up monies to the Child Care Initiative. This program recruited and trained 230 family day care providers, thereby increasing the supply of child care by 1,000 slots. The initiative received more than $1.2 million in funds from 14 corporations and 9 government agencies.

A similar program in New York City, the Neighborhood Child Care Initiatives Project, was begun with funds from American Express foundation and has received approximately $400,000 in funding from 10 corporations. Operated by Child Care Inc., the initiative expects to greatly increase the number of family day care slots throughout the five boroughs.

Gannett Foundation provided the Metropolitan Washington Council of Governments (COG) with a $3,000 grant to help recruit and train 2,000 family day care providers in the Washington, D.C. area.[47]

In New York City, the Agency for Child Development, which operates publicly funded child care programs, has developed a resource and referral capability. One aim of the service is to provide vacancy control and up-to-the-minute information about the availability of programs. The system includes private as well as publicly funded programs.

States and cities throughout the country are recognizing the importance of offering resource and referral services to parents. California, through the creation of the Child Care Resource and Referral Agency, developed a statewide network connecting agencies that already existed and providing them with technical assistance. Connecticut and New Jersey are also developing networks of resource and referral agencies. Cities such as Dallas, Boston, and Minneapolis likewise have resource and referral services.

Identifying the Need

Many resource and referral agencies document requests for care and the response of the agency. Companies that contract with R&Rs can request periodic reports of their own employees' requests and whether these requests were met. This is important information for tracking the specific needs of employees and to see if the R&R is providing the services promised. Worksheet 11 shows the kind of information that can be obtained from resource and referral agency reports.

Frequently, usage of an R&R is low—anywhere from 5 percent on down to one-half of 1 percent of the employee population. The use depends on several factors: how well publicized the program is, how responsive and accessible it is (for example, when the phone lines are open), and the extent of the need at the moment. Most parents who have care stay with what they have, except at turning points in development—for example, when a child turns two and a half or three, at which time parents prefer a center to family day care—or when they move to a new locale. To parents who need care at the moment, the service may be crucial in helping them find a quality program and peace of mind. While at a given time or in a given year the number may not be great, over time a high proportion of employees tend to use the service.

What the Service Can and Cannot Do

Most resource and referral agencies provide information only about state-licensed or registered care. Many do not actually visit or personally screen the programs on their lists. This points up the importance of parents' knowing how to evaluate and choose child care. An employer contracting with such an agency should be sure to find out what kind of monitoring, if any, the vendor does, and what help, if any, parents are given in evaluating care.

Buying Into an Existing System

Throughout the United States, especially in major cities, resource and referral agencies exist that are eager to work with employers. Lotus Development, Shawmut Bank, and Arthur Anderson and Company are among the 33 corporations that contract with Child Care Resource Center in Cambridge, Massachusetts, for employee counseling and information by phone or in person.

In Danbury, Connecticut, the local child care resource and referral service was created when the city of Danbury conducted a survey of the needs of residents. Funded primarily by state monies, start-up also included donations from 5 corporations. Among the corporations that contract with the service are Boehringer Ingelheim. Four corporations, while not contracting directly with the service, donate between $3,000 and $5,000 per year to its operations. The service provides information about child care in the Greater Danbury area, which includes ten towns.

If the local resource and referral agency is not equipped to handle the volume of requests that a corporate contract would mean, monies should be provided to expand the number of counselors and to identify a greater number and range of programs. Care should be taken to find programs whose location and hours meet the needs of your employees.

Pooling Resources—Consortium

A resource and referral service established through the efforts of the Washington Council of Governments pulled together information and referral services in six counties. Each county had a different system. The council became the coordinator of these services, providing a forum and technical assistance to help them expand the services to meet the needs of employees in supporting companies. This project was initiated by BNA, a private publishing firm in Washington, D.C. that contributed $5,000 in start-up money and encouraged other businesses in the Washington area to contribute. The consortium now includes companies in three states. In all, corporations contributed $10,000 and the council matched this to develop the project. Corporations are also providing in-kind services. For example, Giant Supermarkets printed the brochure describing the project in English and Spanish.

Developing a Service In-House

Some employers choose to start their own resource and referral program in-house. In 1980, Steelcase, in Grand Rapids, Michigan, hired two part-time consultants trained in early childhood education. The company, which produces office "environments," is rapidly expanding and now has 8,000 employees in the Greater Grand Rapids area.

The company gradually expanded the service. It is now staffed by two full-time and one part-time consultant. They provide extensive face-to-face counseling to families, helping them assess their child care needs and choose infant, day, evening, and after-school care and babysitting.

Since local programs could not meet the expressed demand for infant care, the consultants developed a family day care network. The network now has between 300 and 400 registered family day care homes, which are available to community families as well as Steelcase employees. Participating providers attend training workshops, can borrow cribs, playpens and other equipment as well as books, and receive a newsletter from the consultants.

Deb VanderMolen, one of the consultants, reports that usage of the program has increased eightfold during the years from 1980 to 1986. In 1986, more than 500 children were placed in care. The keystone of the program is its personal approach to families and caregivers. The consultants educate both groups to understand quality child care. At parents' requests, they will work with in-home caregivers, helping them develop their skills in early childhood.

Of employees who used the program, the following were their reasons:

—46 percent were returning to work;

—9 percent had providers who stopped the arrangement;

—6 percent had personality conflicts with their provider;

—5 percent had a change in work hours;

—5 percent needed temporary child care;

—5 percent had moved; and

—24 percent had other reasons (not recorded).

At Kaiser Permanente in Los Angeles, California, a Child Care Coordinator provides employees with a child care directory, which she updates yearly. The coordinator is also on-site at the largest location twice a week to answer employees' questions either face to face or by telephone. Kaiser Permanente has 20,000 employees in Southern California. About 800 of the 4,600 eligible employees make use of the program, which grew out of labor/management negotiations.[48]

A feasibility study of employees' needs, conducted by the author for a hospital in Texas, found that although there was ample child care during the day, finding care for the evening hours and on weekends was a big problem for employees. The hospital decided to develop an in-house resource and referral program to identify family day care homes and centers that could provide care for employees during shift hours.

How To Start

To plan a resource and referral service, you should work with a professional who knows the child care system. Consultants can begin by contacting resources in the community where the company is located or where parents live. To get an initial list of services, contact the Department of Social Services or Department of Health, depending on whichever agency licenses programs in your area. Also contact women's, child care, and other professional organizations (such as the National Association for the Education of Young Children [NAEYC]), public schools, and other employers to find out if they use any form of resource and referral. You will need to determine what services exist, both licensed and unlicensed, and how accessible they are. If you have difficulty finding them, you can be sure parents are also struggling to do so. Use Worksheet 12 to record all pertinent information.

Liability

It is understandable that many employers are concerned about the liability of offering a child care service, particularly one that is hard to monitor. Employers, concerned that they have "deep pockets" (compared to resource and referral agencies) would want to protect themselves when referral agencies and providers fail to offer a high level of protection.

While the decision to accept the risk of providing resource and referral should be made with the advice of legal counsel, there are ways of limiting risk to the employer.

According to Catalyst, the following should be observed:

1. Clearly state that only information and advice are given, and not recommendations or endorsements of particular providers. Many services provide at least two references.

2. Make sure parents understand that they have a choice even if names of programs are given.

3. State in a written disclaimer that the company takes no responsibility for the service, and make sure this is printed on all publications.

4. Have a policy for complaints and letting parents and providers know the procedures and what action will be taken.

5. Check to see if family day care centers have their own liability insurance and do not list them if they do not.

6. Have legal counsel determine the feasibility of adding liability insurance to existing corporate coverage (in most cases, this will not be difficult, especially if the company already supports rehabilitation programs, EAPs, etc.).[49]

Perhaps the best way to avoid problems is to be sure the service you offer and the programs you are involved with are of the highest quality. Few high-quality programs have liability claims, let alone judgments against them. Programs that have been credentialed by recognized authorities such as the National Association for the Education of Young Children or that receive ongoing training are those that can be best trusted to provide consistently high quality care. (See Chapter 6 for more information about quality care.)

Worksheet 6
Management Perspective: Charitable Contributions

A company's philosophy influences its choice of child care options. You can also build on the company's relationship with an existing community agency. This chart can help you determine what option(s) might be best for your company.

List community agencies and programs (United Way, etc.) that the company contributes to. Check with the corporate contributions department.

Name of Agency/Address

e.g. YM-YWCA

Function of Agency

Provides athletic and social programs for children and families in the community.

Amount of Donation

$5,000

Date

7/14/87

Indicate the type and amount of support you provide for each child care service. As you find out more about the specific child care needs of your employees, you can adjust this support.

Name of Program/Address

Type of Support (purchase of slots, in-kind services, charitable contributions, etc.)

Number of Parent Users

Job Titles

Cost

Parent Satisfaction

Problems/Suggestions

Date

Worksheet 8
Preparation of Workshops/Seminars

Use the following information to plan workshops or seminars.

A. List topics of interest to employees who have (or are planning to have) children.

1. Balancing career and family

2.

B. List workshop leaders who are available to conduct sessions.

Name Affiliation Address/Phone Speciality Fee Reference

C. Suggested budget for sessions

D. Time schedule – preferred day, time, month, etc.

E. Location

F. Number of employees/how grouped for the sessions

G. Comments

Sample Workshop Notice and Sign-up Form

[Post or distribute notices to employees about planned workshops or seminars.]

To: All Widget employees

From: Jane Smith, Human Resources

Re: Lunchtime Workshop
   Topic: "Taking the Sting Out of Parental Guilt."

Widget has scheduled our first Working Parent Lunchtime Workshop. The session will be conducted by Mary Jones of X Consultants, a specialist in the needs of working parents.

The discussion will focus on:
 - How do children fare when their parents work?

 - Five ways to get rid of guilt

The Workshop is scheduled for Wednesday, February 10 at 12:00 noon until 1:00 p.m. in the third floor training room. Feel free to bring your lunch. Soft drinks will be provided.

Space is limited so please fill out the attached form and return it no later than January 20 to: Jane Smith, Human Resources.

____Yes, I would like to attend the session, "TAKING THE STING OUT OF PARENTAL GUILT," scheduled for Wednesday, February 10, 1988, 12:00 noon to 1:00 p.m.

____I would like to attend but cannot. A better day for me is_____

Name_____Office Ext._____

Ages of Children_____Department_____

Home Address_____

What other topics are you interested in?_____

Following are two options for employer feedback of workshops. Choose the type that best suits your corporate style.

A. Feedback Sheet

1. What did you like most about the session?

2. What did you like least?

3. Suggestions for future session:

B. Feedback Sheet

1) How useful was the session?

____Very useful   ____Somewhat useful   ____Not useful

2) How would you rate the group leader?

____Very good   ____Somewhat good   ____Not good

3) Would you attend another session conducted by the leader?

____Yes   ____Maybe   ____No   ____Depends on the topic

4) Comments:

Worksheet 10
Child Care Resource and Referral Agencies

Record information about organizations that list child care programs.
Include all types of child care programs (centers, family day care,
before/after school care, summer programs, etc.) both public and private.

			Types of Programs Listed	Geog.Area Covered	No.of Slots	How Monitored	Reports/ Frequency	Fees
Name	Address	Contact						

You can also include: Additional services offered, such as workshops,
counseling, etc.

Worksheet 11
Child Care Resource and Referral Report

Record specific information requested and selected by employees.

Request Date	Employee Job Categ.	Community	Family Income	Ages of Chldrn	Days/Hrs for Service	Type of Prog. Requested	Outcome/ Date

Worksheet 12
Profile of Specific Child Care Programs

This form can be the basis for an in-house resource and referral service, voucher program, corporate donation, etc. Contact child care providers (centers, family day care networks, in-home care agencies, etc.) and record information about each on a separate sheet. Be sure to include the reactions of parents using the service.

Name of Program_____Contact Person/Title_____

Address_____Phone_____

Type of Service_____Dates Contacted_____

Contacted by_____

Sponsoring Organization_____When Started_____

Type of Corporate Entity (Non-profit, proprietary, etc.)_____

License No./Date_____ No. of Slots_____

Ages of Children_____Groupings_____

Hours_____Fees_____Food Service_____

Transportation_____Openings/Waiting List_____

Adult/Child Ratios_____

Staff Credentials/Training_____

Staff Turnover_____

Insurance Coverage_____

Reactions of Parents Using the Service_____

_____

(Include name, extension no., date)

Reactions of Consultant/Observer_____

_____

(Include name, position, date of observation, comments)

NOTES

1. Ellen Galinsky, Diane Hughes, and Marybeth Shinn, "Work and Family Life Study Pinpoints Sources of Stress for Corporate Workers," *Family Resource Coalition Report*, Vol. 5, No. 2, 1986, pp. 7-9.

2. "Alternative Work Schedules Becoming More Favorable," p. 4.

3. Clifford Baden and Dana Friedman, *New Management Initiatives for Working Parents*, Boston: Wheelock College, 1981, p. 90.

4. Ibid., p. 91.

5. Bureau of National Affairs, *Work and Family: A Changing Dynamic*, pp. 68-69.

6. "Flexible Work Schedules and Staffing Increase," p. 4.

7. U.S. Department of Labor, *Facts on U.S. Working Women*, p. 1.

8. "Workplace Alternatives," p. 130.

9. U.S. Department of Labor, *Facts on U.S. Working Women*, p. 2.

10. U.S. Department of Labor, *Facts on U.S. Working Women*, p. 3.

11. "Workplace Alternatives," p. 130.

12. U.S. Department of Labor, *Facts on U.S. Working Women*, p. 3.

13. Ibid.

14. Ibid.

15. Kotlowitz, "Working At Home While Caring for Child Sounds Fine," p. 21.

16. Christensen, "A National Study of Home-Based Work," p. 8.

17. Ibid.

18. Kotlowitz, "Working At Home," p. 21.

19. U.S. Department of Labor, *Facts on U.S. Working Women*, p. 4.

20. Ibid.

21. Bureau of National Affairs, *Work and Family*, p. 156.

22. Galinsky, Hughes, and Shinn, "Work and Family Life," p. 9.

23. Ibid., p. 8.

24. Kamerman, *Meeting Family Needs*, p. 8.

25. "Pregnancy Leave Practices," p. 78.

26. Ibid., p. 101.

27. Ibid.

28. Ibid.

29. Bureau of National Affairs, "Pregnancy and Employment: Problems and Progress," p. 101.

30. Michel McQueen, "States Set Pace on Innovative Laws for Child Care," p. 72.

31. "Mandatory Maternal," *The Wall Street Journal*, July 21, 1987, p. 1.

32. "Pregnancy and Employment," p. 102.

33. Bureau of National Affairs, *Work and Family*, p. 106.

34. Ibid., p. 107.

35. *The Corporate Guide to Parental Leaves*, p. 45.

36. Bureau of National Affairs, *Work and Family*, pp. 119-120.

37. Ibid.

38. U.S. Department of Labor, Bureau of Labor Statistics, "Employee Benefits in Medium and Large Firms," July 1986, p. 82.

39. Friedman, "Special Report," p. 12.

40. "Flexible Compensation: Women Favor Programs More Than Men, ECFC Employee Attitude Survey Finds," *BNA Pension Reporter*, Vol. 14, March 16, 1987, p. 320.

41. Sterling North, "Voucher System Helps Companies Administer Benefits for Child Care," *New England Business*, March 16, 1987, p. 35.

42. "Voucher Programs for Child Care Help Employees," *Employee Benefit Plan Review*, September 1987, p. 26.

43. "Maximum Employee Choice at Minimal Employer Effort," *Day Care USA*, October 27, 1986, Vol. 15, No. 23.

44. Bureau of National Affairs, *Work and Family*, p. 45.

45. Collins, "Day Care Finds Corporate Help," p. B5.

46. Ibid.

47. "In Brief." *Day Care USA*, Vol. 15, No. 124, November 10, 1986, p. 4.

48. Bureau of National Affairs, *Work and Family*, p. 56.

49. Catalyst Career and Family Center, "Child Care Information Service," p. 13.

4

HOW EMPLOYERS SUPPORT WORKING PARENTS: PART II

DEVELOPMENT OF NEW CHILD CARE PROGRAMS

Employers may support the development of new child care programs after careful examination of employees' needs, the company's goals, and the community's resources. The development of a new program can take many forms. In some cases, the success of previous efforts prompts this development. For example, Steelcase created its family day care network after its fruitful involvement with a child care resource and referral agency.

Other initiatives that employers have developed include on- or near-site child care centers, family day care networks, consortium networks, before- and after-school programs, care for sick children, and emergency or "drop in" care.

Child Care Centers

The most visible option is the development of a child care center at or near the work site. Such programs tend to be useful in recruiting and retaining employees, more so than resource and referral programs, according to one study.[1]

Center care is increasing at a faster rate than either family day care or in-home care. Center care is becoming an important option for infants and toddlers as well as preschoolers (three- to five-year-olds) whose mothers work full-time.[2]

Although only a small percentage of corporations are involved in such centers, the number is increasing dramatically. According to Kathryn Perry's research, in 1978 there were 25 corporate child care centers in operation, excluding hospitals and universities.[3] This number almost doubled by 1983, when the National Employer-Supported Child Care Study was completed.

Figures from the Conference Board for 1987 place the number at approximately 150, a threefold increase.

By far the largest and fastest growth has been in hospitals. In 1987, 100 child care centers were found in health care institutions. By 1983, there were about 300, and by 1986 more than 500, according to the National Association of Hospital-Affiliated Child Care Programs. This amounts to a growth rate of 500 percent in eight years.

Most experts agree that these figures are not definitive. Not only do new programs appear daily, but many existing ones are not publicized (many employers like to stay out of the limelight). For example, a small company in New York City operated an on-site child care center for employees' children for three years without publicity. Despite the fact that the employees and the center staff were delighted with the program, management viewed the program primarily as a service to employees. Another concern was that if the general public knew about the center, the company would be deluged with visitors and applicants.

An unusual center was created by the owner of a small office-cleaning service in Texas. Faced with high absenteeism and turnover, she realized that child care might make the difference in keeping her best employees. She bought a house adjacent to her office, renovated it, and offered it rent-free to anyone trained in early childhood education who would be willing to care for the children of her employees.

As with other educational institutions, employer-supported child care centers can change. Unfortunately, a few companies have withdrawn support for a center, either because of financial hardship, being acquired by another corporation, or because operations were shut down at the particular location.

Starting in August 1984, Howard Johnson supported a child center in Quincy, Massachusetts until the company was bought out at the end of 1985. The new employer did not want to continue the center. Parents pulled together and turned the center into a nonprofit corporation (it had been a division of Howard Johnson), established credit with a local bank, and raised funds to continue the program.

More often, however, programs expand, offering care to more children and new age groups. Kid Korral Day Care Center, in Binghamton, New York, serves the children of New York State employees, and originally offered care only to young children. Recently, however, it began offering after-school care and full-time summer care for school-age children. Fel Pro, which at first offered school-age summer care, expanded into day care for young children. Wang Labs, which originally offered care only for preschoolers, added infant and school-age care.

Some programs change in response to new needs. Centenella Child Care Center, which is a division of Centenella Hospital, originally served only employees of the hospital. Recently, the program became available to employees of other local institutions.

A strong child care center is one that is responsive to changing needs, while maintaining a quality program.

Corporate Affiliation

An on-site center can be affiliated with a company in several different ways. It can be owned and operated by the company, owned by the company and managed by an outside group, or owned and operated by an outside group, such as a nonprofit agency or a for-profit company. The choice depends on administrative and legal considerations.

Although each on-site center is unique (because each situation is unique), a study of 15 industrial centers and 30 educational centers came up with the following criteria for a successful on-site child care center:

—Commitment from a major corporation or other sponsor (such as a foundation), including long-range financial support;
—Qualified, trained, adequately paid staff members;
—Realistic expectations about profit-making potential and effects on employees;
—Realistic expectations about enrollment (expecting only 5 to 10 percent of families who indicated interest on original survey);
—A comprehensive program including education and attention to health.[4]

The recipe for a successful center usually begins with an adequate market analysis or assessment of employee needs, a careful look at the goals of the company and the services offered in the community, involvement of parent/ users in the plans for the program and in the ongoing operation, the development of a quality program for children, and ongoing assessment.

Some Considerations about On- or Near-Site Centers

For large employers of highly skilled professionals or whose work force consists of large numbers of women, an on- or near-site center may help in recruitment and retention. Women may return from maternity leave sooner if their children are cared for near their work. Absenteeism and lateness may be cut considerably if parents do not have to rely on unpredictable caregivers who may be late or ill.

With company support and resources, child care centers have the capability to offer the highest quality child care programs. High quality child care centers within corporations are good for morale. There is a humanizing of the work place, a sense of caring. Most employees feel proud of companies that have child care centers. If the company's product or service is child- or family-related, the center can also be used for research or promotion of the product.

However, a high-quality center that cannot accommodate all employees who need the care can result in employee frustration. An executive who could not get her child into her company-sponsored center eventually left the company in anger. Enrollment policies have to be considered carefully. In the afore-mentioned case, management decided that, although the loss of the executive was an unhappy one for the company, the overall goals and philosophy dictated that enrollment be on a first come, first served basis. One way of dealing with this was to expand the supply of care to accommodate all families in need. When the waiting list for the Campbell Soup Center reached 90, the company decided to expand the program from 118 to 295 children.[5] Besides quality, cost is a factor in the demand for a program. Those that are heavily subsidized and charge parents below the going rate in the community, tend to be in greatest demand.

There are other problems and challenges posed by employer-supported child care centers. In one center, an episode in which one young child bit another (not unknown in child care) was blown out of proportion. Soon all the employees had heard of the incident and knew who the parent of the "biting" child was. This caused the parent embarrassment and concern. It is essential that the privacy of parents be protected and confidentiality maintained.

When a center is located near the work site, one benefit is that parents can visit their children during lunch and breaks. This tends to encourage staff to provide the highest quality care. Since a child with a problem may be more "visible," all parents should be cautioned against sharing personal information about fellow parents with other employees.

A center may be created with built-in flexibility, so that it responds to the changing needs of the families it serves. It can begin as a preschool, expand to include infants, and later add on care for school-age children (before- and after-school and during holidays). It can also be the basis of a summer camp. With careful planning, the space can be converted back to offices if it is no longer needed for children. There are a number of reasons why a center may not be appropriate for your company at this time. Space may be at a premium—too little or too costly—or parents who have a long commute on public trans-portation may be reluctant to bring young children with them. There may be services near their homes that would be more appropriate. Most companies do not want to duplicate services and compete with community programs.

Liability

During the last several years, child care programs throughout the country have experienced massive increases in the cost of liability insurance. In many cases, premiums were cancelled with little or no warning to providers. A 1986 survey of child care providers throughout the country found that nearly two-thirds of family day care homes and more than one-third of centers could not renew their liability insurance or had had it canceled. In addition, almost 60 percent had received rate increases during the year. For more than half of the programs, the increase was more than double their premium.[6]

There are several reasons for this crisis. One is that carriers report that insuring child care is not cost-effective. Another is that child abuse claims, although few, have raised fear and distrust among insurers.

Many experts believe that the concern of insurers is unwarranted. They point out that 90 percent of child care providers have never had a claim filed against them. Of those who have, 80 percent report claims totaling less than $500.[7]

Ours is frequently called a "litigious" society. Many professionals, notably physicians, have received great increases in liability insurance premiums, in part because of the costly malpractice judgments against some. It is not surprising that the employers who are considering supporting child care centers are concerned about liability.

There are several ways of reducing the company's exposure to liability. Most important is to be associated only with a program that is of the highest quality, since such programs have few accidents, few law suits, and few judgments against them. Some employers, such as Dominion Bankshares, believe that quality is more easily maintained by setting the center up as a division of the company, and making center staff company employees.

Others, such as Johnson Wax, choose to have a nonprofit child care agency own and operate the service. The company believes that the provider, having been in the child care business for some time, is more likely to know what "quality" is and how to maintain it. Either way, the corporation must take responsibility for the quality, elicit parent feedback, and do its own monitoring.

Liability exposure is limited by an "arm's-length" relationship with the provider. As a separate corporation, which owns the building and the program, the provider is the first to shoulder the responsibility, as in the case of the Johnson Wax program. Joanne Brandis, an attorney who helped found the center, states that the provider of the service should have ample insurance and should indemnify the company against liability.

Companies pay anywhere between $2,500 and $12,000 per year for liability insurance, depending on the location and extent to which safety factors are met. The Official Airline Guide Center pays $5,000 per year for a general liability insurance policy.

Jim Strickland works for Human Services Risk Management Exchange in Austin, Texas, an organization that specializes in loss control training. He reports that employers should also consider vehicle insurance, because most children get transported at some time during the day. He says that this insurance, however, is most variable in cost.

Some insurers are willing to provide child care insurance coverage to a corporation at reasonable cost, especially if they carry other policies for the company.

Marketdyne, a division of Cigna, is now writing policies for members of the National Association for the Education of Young Children at reasonable rates. Insurers of child care centers are more stringent than they used to be in their requirements for coverage. For example, many require higher adult:child ratios than state regulations require, and demand facilities with well-designed exits, sprinkler systems, and so on. Staff also must have a plan for emergency evacuation, and must practice periodically. Such requirements are well worth their extra cost, as they create safer environments for children.

Planning a Program

Once you decide that a child care center is a possibility for your company, you still need to consider the specifics of a program.

Organization.   Programs are usually organized by age groups—infants (0 to 15 months), toddlers (16 to 31 months), and preschool (31 months to 5 years). You may also want to consider kindergarten, which usually covers ages 5 to 6. Child care centers are licensed by state, city, and/or local agencies. There are specific regulations about space, health, safety, staffing, group size, and so forth, that must be considered.

Usually, regulations are based on minimum standards. Most agencies also have "suggested" or "recommended" standards that are slightly more stringent. We urge you to consider these standards, since they are more likely to promote safety and quality.

Contact agencies that license child care in your state (see Appendix A). Worksheet 13 can help you keep track of program requirements.

According to a 1980 study of employer-supported child care centers, such centers tended to have certain characteristics:

- Ninety percent of the centers were on site.
- Most served infants, preschoolers, and school-age children.
- Eighty percent served only children of company employees.
- A few served children of people employed nearby or in the community.
- Most operated from 6 A.M. to 8 P.M. (with many hospitals offering double shift hours to midnight).
- Operating expenses at most centers were covered by parent tuition with some company subsidies. In some cases, the company accepted almost full responsibility for the cost of operating the center.
- Companies subsidized centers in many ways: 71 percent provided the building, 53 percent provided start-up costs, 43 percent provided materials, 42 percent subsidized overhead costs (rent, utilities, and so on) and 36 percent received government money.[8]

Since the time of this study, not only have many new centers been developed, but many have changed. Several programs that initially enrolled only children of employees have begun accepting children from the community or whose parents are employed at other companies. Lenore Schrag of Centinella Hospital Center reports that as children grow up, the policy of opening up the center to community children but still having slots for employees' children will be a good one.

How to Create a Center

For this discussion, refer to Worksheets 14 and 15.

Deciding on Space Requirements.   Use Worksheet 14 to analyze the space you will need to create a center. The answers to Items 1 and 2 will come from an employee needs assessment, whether formally or informally done. Write the responses to Item 1 in the correct columns in Item 4 in Worksheet 14. Now refer to Worksheet 13 to find the amount of square footage needed per child according to age. Record this in Item 4 in Worksheet 14 and multiply the figures to calculate the space requirements.

Identifying Possible Sites.   You should visit possible sites with your consultant, a licensing agent, or other expert in early childhood education. Look for public schools that are underenrolled, office space on low floors, buildings owned by the company, small houses, and so forth. The consultant can point out areas that will need adaptation or additional construction. Consider access to major roads or public transportation, particularly if the site is not directly adjacent to the company. Be sure that if parents are driving, there is a place for them to park their cars when they drop off their children.

A contractor can help determine the cost per square foot for renovation. If possible, talk to one who has had experience with child care centers since these pose problems that other types of buildings do not. Look for space that can be expanded. List the advantages and disadvantages of each possible site. Consider ways to reduce the cost of space, for example by providing child care for other tenants in the building.

Capital outlay for building or modifying the site will vary, depending on the facility. You must consider the plumbing, lighting, heat, fire exits, and so on. It is very important to involve child care experts in the planning of the facility. One company used an in-house architect to draw up plans for a proposed center. A review of the plans found that unnecessary space had been added in some cases, while essential space (bathrooms) had been overlooked. Also, far more space had been allocated than was necessary, because per person calculations included adults as well as children. If you are lucky, existing space can be adapted with minor adjustments. Again, community licensing agencies, child care specialists, and insurance agents specializing in child care centers can be of assistance.

Selecting Staff.   Regulations and guidelines governing staff selection may be issued by different agencies in different communities (see Appendix A). These guidelines cover age restrictions and educational requirements for caregivers as well as the number of children of a given age that can be cared for by one caregiver (ratio of children to adults). Since younger children need more adult attention, the ratio of adults to children is higher for very young children. (See Chapter 5 for more information about ratios and what qualifications to look for in caregivers.)

Regulations also determine how many children of each age can be grouped together. As mentioned earlier, licensing departments often have literature describing not only "required" but "suggested" ratios and educational backgrounds. It is advisable to lean toward the suggested or added requirements to enhance the quality of the program.

In some states, caregivers must be fingerprinted and checked for criminal records. You may want to check your state licensing department's policies.

Child care is labor-intensive. Salaries typically represent 70 to 80 percent of any child care center's budget. The National Day Care Study and recent research indicate that cutting costs by reducing the staff-to-child ratio and relaxing standards for teacher qualifications has a negative impact on the quality of a program. Conversely, upgrading staff through higher salaries and training can contribute significantly to the quality of care and may be well worth the investment (see Chapter 5).[9]

Setting Salaries.   Unfortunately, child care providers are poorly paid, particularly in comparison with public school elementary and high-school teachers. In some cases, companies can provide benefit packages that upgrade total compensation. If the child care staff is employed directly by the company, salaries will probably be consistent with other company employees.

In Worksheet 14 (which provides space for a rough estimate of staffing costs), be sure to include benefits, recruitment, staff development (training), and substitute costs (approximately another 15 percent).

Materials and Equipment—Program Costs.   The consultant can help you estimate program costs. Start-up costs will cover such items as furniture and outdoor and indoor play equipment. Consumables (toys, paper, paints, and so on), although not a substantial outlay, must be figured into ongoing or operational costs. Supplies such as cribs and special outdoor equipment must also be planned for younger children.

Start-up costs for employer-supported on-site centers vary considerably, depending on whether a facility is to be built from the ground up (the most expensive) or whether only minor renovations are indicated. The amount can be as low as $50,000 or as high as $1 million. Included are a survey of employee needs, professional planning and preparation, equipping a center, staff recruitment, and publicity. Worksheet 15 will help you analyze start-up costs.

Figuring Operating Costs.   The number of days of actual operation must be considered. Many programs "over enroll" because they are aware that on any given day a certain percentage of children will be absent. However, even when children are absent, your operational expenses will not vary substantially, since staff is constant and 70 to 80 percent of your cost is for personnel. You must also be aware of the effect on program costs of hours of operation (how many shifts, holidays, closings for other reasons, and so on). Although program costs can be reduced by high enrollment owing to economies of scale, you must be careful not to compromise quality. Optimally, a center should have between 25 and 75 children. If there are more, space should be designed to give a feeling of intimacy. Maintenance and certain housekeeping functions need to be included in program costs.

Financing a Center—Employer Contribution.   Both the amount and the timing of the employer's contribution to an on- or near-site center can be planned to meet the employer's needs as well as those of the child care program. Some possibilities for financing a center—whole or in part—include in-kind contributions, a one-time contribution, a low-interest loan for startup and capital outlay, and a commitment to a fixed percentage of employees' child care costs.

Employer contributions to the planning and development of a child care center often do not appear in the budget of the center. These contributions vary depending on what a company can offer in the way of services and materials. According to the 1978 study by Kathryn Perry, employers subsidized their centers with a variety of in-kind services: 78 percent gave free use of the facility, 53 percent gave janitor services, 36 percent gave food service, 45 percent gave health services, 27 percent gave secretarial services, 20 percent gave maintenance and repair service, 5 percent gave laundry, 17 percent gave utilities, and 16 percent gave other services.[10]

In some cases, as in most government-supported centers, employers make a one-time contribution to help start a center, and may also provide rent, utilities and maintenance services free of charge. This enables the center to charge lower parent fees, thereby offering care to families who would not otherwise be able to afford the center. Employers sometimes make a low-interest loan available to a particular group. With this to help cover start-up costs, parent tuitions may be able to cover the costs of operation.

Many employers choose to pay a percentage of the cost of care for each employee. If the care costs $60 per child per week, the employer may decide to subsidize 50 percent, or $30 per child. Worksheet 14 will help you assess the amount of money the company will have to invest in the center. Parent employees can have fees deducted from their salaries, through a dependent care assistance plan funded by salary reduction (see Chapter 3). In this way, the company also benefits as it does not pay social security, unemployment, or other payroll taxes on that money.

Financing a Center—Obtaining a Low-Interest Loan.   A number of banks are providing low-interest loans to employer-supported child care centers. In this case, the employer may choose to provide operating monies rather than start-up.

How to Figure Parent Tuition Fees.   In general, we recommend that parents pay a fee for the service provided. The amount that parents pay will depend on several factors, including family income and what percentage of the cost of care the company wants to subsidize. If many parents are single and earning under $20,000, the company may choose to subsidize a large part of the operation. If the center is used by families representing a range of incomes, those who are in a high income bracket (typically two-career families) may be asked to pay more than the average cost per child, while those in low brackets may pay less.

To help you determine fees, look at what similar services in your community charge. For example, if care for preschool children in your community costs between $35 and $45 per child per week, you will want to price your service accordingly. The actual cost of care for infants and toddlers is higher than for older children because younger children require a higher staff ratio. Operating costs for employer-supported centers serving about 50 children can run between $150,000 and $300,000 per year or more. This means that the cost of care per child in these programs is between $3,000 and $6,000 per year.

Putting It All Together—Getting Expert Advice.   The development and management of an employer-supported child care center is complicated. In some cases, years may pass between the time that initial steps are taken and the opening of a center. Hiring an individual to coordinate and implement the necessary steps can greatly facilitate the process. (See Worksheets 13 and 14 and end of chapter.)

Examples of Centers Sponsored by Individual Companies

Institute for Scientific Information (near site)—Philadelphia, Pennsylvania. ISI, a company that uses computers to gather and disseminate information, employs 450 people, mostly women, in the Philadelphia area. Adjacent to its own busy downtown site, ISI developed the $1.5 million ISI Caring Center for Children and Parents. Opened in the fall of 1982, the center was designed to serve not just ISI employees but other businesses and hospitals in the area.

Operated as a subsidiary of ISI, the center cares for up to 160 children— infants through kindergarteners—and has a small summer camp program for preschoolers and young school-age children. While care used to be provided at night, the usage was too low to be cost-effective. Hours are from 7 A.M. to 6 P.M. Fees range from $172 per week for infants to $118 per week for preschoolers. Meals and snacks are included.

Approximately 12 percent of the parents are ISI employees. The downtown, central location enables parents from nearby universities, hospitals, and other large employer sites to use the program. Susan Silverstein, who has been the director since the program's inception, reports that her studies have found that parents use the ISI center because they prefer to have their children near them during the workday.

According to ISI officials, "The center [was] built not just for our present employees, but specifically for our future employees—in recognition of the dramatic changes in the demographics of our society projected over the remainder of this century."[11]

Corning Glass (near site)—Corning, New York.   The Corning Glass Works Foundation funded a task force study of the needs of 8,000 parents in Corning, New York. A survey was conducted to determine the need for a center.

The foundation provided a grant of $40,000 for the start-up of the center. An additional $4,000 was provided for an information and referral service. During the first year of operation, care was provided for 24 children aged three to five years at a cost of $55 per child per week, of which the foundation subsidized $17 per child per week. At a fee of $45 per child (whether Corning family or community family) the Corning Foundation provides a $34,200 subsidy of the program. Between one-half and two-thirds of the children have parents who are employed at Corning. The rest come from the community. The board of directors consists of Corning management personnel, parents, and residents. The center is seen as a joint venture of the foundation and the community.

Official Airline Guides (on site)—Oak Brook, Illinois. Official Airline Guides, Inc. (OAG) is a company that publishes data for transportation. The firm is more than 70 percent female, and employees are not highly paid. The center was developed in 1981 by the original owner of OAG, the R.H. Donnelly Publishing Company. The president, James W. Woodward, initiated the center to help recruit and retain employees in a highly competitive industry. In fact, about half of the employees have been with the company for five years or more.

The community is suburban and the building was a new facility. One vice-president explored space feasibility, and Susan Doctors, manager of Human Resources, worked with a consultant to design and develop the program.

Set up as a division of the company, the center cares for 71 children, ages three months to five years, from 7 A.M. to 6 P.M. The ratio of adults to infants is one to four, to toddlers one to five, and to preschoolers one to eight. Fourteen teachers are on staff, and are paid wages and benefits comparable with those of other OAG employees. Fees range from $62 per week for three- and four-year olds to $100 per week for infants. The rest of the cost of care is absorbed by the company, which provides the space, janitorial services, and food. The company's experience is that the center "does have a positive impact on employee loyalty to the company. Employees tend to stay with [the] company and to recommend the company to prospective employees because of the center."[12]

Other benefits are that employees are more likely to return to work after maternity leave and, by being nearby in case of emergency, and by knowing and trusting the staff, employees are able to focus on work.

Dominion Bankshares Corporation (on site)—Roanoke, Virginia. A child care feasibility study conducted by an employee for a management training class received high praise. When the study was shown to Warner Dalhouse, the president, he decided to go ahead with a center. A survey of nearly 800 employees (almost 1,000 are at the site) found that more than half had difficulty obtaining child care that met their needs. Almost 60 percent reported that, as working mothers, they were stressed by child care problems. High absenteeism and turnover were also associated with child care problems.[13]

The center, which began operating in 1986, serves 70 children ages six weeks to five years. Care costs parents $40 per week for children over two and $65 per week for children under two. The company subsidy, which is 50 percent, amounts to about $85,000 per year. The center is a division of the corporation. The 19 staff members are Dominion employees and receive salary and benefits from the company.

The center also offers parenting seminars and resource and referral. "Morale of the entire company seems to be affected positively, even though only a relatively few people actually use the center."[14]

Campbell Soup Company, Camden, New Jersey.   The center came about when two female employees asked the president for on-site child care. A survey indicated a need. Initially, the center was operated by Kindercare. However, Resources for Child Care Management, a child care management firm, now operates the program.

The center serves 120 children ages six months through kindergarten. Parents pay $33.50 per week for older children and $48 per week for younger children. The company subsidizes the program by 50 percent.

Programs Sponsored by Government Agencies

Federal Government.   Child care programs initiated by federal agencies vary in scope, number of children served, costs, parent fees and involvement, services provided by the agency, and authority under which they were established. The General Accounting Office ruled in 1976 that upon determination that such services were necessary for employee welfare and morale, an agency head could provide a program. Arlene Altman, director of the Senate Child Care Center and initiator of the Congressional and Federal Child Care Directors' Association, reports that with passage of legislation in 1987 and further removal of barriers to developing child care centers, she expects that many new federal child care centers will be developed in the next few years. The bill allows for the creation of centers in the same way that credit unions are established among federal agency employees. There are now approximately 26 child care centers sponsored by federal agencies in the Washington, D.C. area and in other parts of the country, such as California and Boston.[15] Several agencies are in the process of planning centers including, for example, the Internal Revenue Service.

Some of these centers also carry out demonstration/research activities in child development, employee stability, and employee career development.

The trend in federal agency child care is toward parent operation and control of a center after an initial period of agency support. All of the centers are operated by nonprofit, primarily parent-run corporations in space usually donated by the agency. The centers are therefore eligible for grants and subsidies from the government agencies as well as in-kind contributions. All of these centers try to have a racial and socioeconomic mix. They use a sliding scale for tuition fees and conduct fund-raising for scholarships. Enrollment in all government centers is limited by available space, and there can be long waiting lists.

Examples of Centers Sponsored by Federal Agencies/Entities

National Institutes of Health (NIH), Bethesda, Maryland.   Begun in June 1973, the NIH Preschool Development program is a separate, nonprofit corporation, housed on the NIH campus. The center cares for 65 children, two and a half to five years old, from 7:30 A.M. to 6:00 P.M. from Monday through Friday. Parents pay on a sliding scale, from $68 to $103 per week depending on income.

With 10,000 employees, NIH is the largest employer in Montgomery County. While the center is now open to children from the community, the overwhelming majority of children are from NIH families. Pat Gokey, who codirects the center with Vanessa Fuss, points out two interesting aspects of the program: (1) Children are grouped the way they are in families—heterogeneously—rather than by age ("interage grouping"). It is felt that care by the same teacher throughout their years at the center helps them feel secure. (2) The program has a strong international feeling, since children come from countries throughout the world.

The turnover rate of teachers is low. One reason cited is that teachers' salaries are higher than the going rate in the community. NIH provides the space and in-kind services, such as maintenance and upkeep.

ChildKind is an infant-toddler center also housed on the NIH campus. Unlike the NIH Preschool Development Center, however, the program is not currently affiliated with NIH. The center is a parent coop, with most members NIH employees.

U.S. Senate (near site)—Washington, D.C. The idea for the center was initiated by parents who work at the Senate and spearheaded by Senator Dennis DeConcini of Arizona and his wife. The center opened in February 1984 in the old Immigration building across the street from the Senate. In May 1986, the center was moved into a new building, a prefab module which cost $170,000 to build. Monies came from the redirection of rehab funds.

The center is under "parent governance." It is a parent-owned, parent-operated cooperative. Arlene Altman, the director, describes the organization as "the old coop model brought up to date" in that "parents are involved in tasks that suit the needs and desires of our families," such as laundry, purchasing, and nap assignments. She says that the model is "unique and important in blending the parent and the work site." Other federal agency centers are also using this model.

The center serves 50 children, ages 18 months to 5 years. In 1987, it began a summer program for 5- to 8-year-olds. Plans are being made to take infants.

Since one goal of the center is to function in a fiscally responsible way, the cost of care is high—from $105 per week for preschoolers up to $125 per week for the youngest children. However, scholarships are available because of the fund-raising efforts of parents. The center can care for children up to 9½ hours each day, and is open from 7:30 A.M. to 6:45 P.M. Following the government calendar, the center is only closed on government holidays.

Priority is given to the children of Senate employees (and members), then to federal agency employees, and finally to the community at large. Currently, the program is filled by Senate employees and has a waiting list of over 100.

State Governments. Many states, including Arizona, California, Florida, Michigan, New York, New Jersey, and Massachusetts have established centers for state employees. Of these, New York has the most extensive on-site program, with 31 centers throughout the state and many more in the planning stage. The state set up the Empire State Day Care Corporation (ESDCC) to oversee the centers. Monies for start-up and ongoing training and program development are funneled through a joint labor management committee. Start-up funds are $19,550 for a program for 30 children, with an additional $350 per child beyond the initial 30. A supplement is provided to centers serving more than 80. All told, since 1979, $4 million has been made available for the network.

The state provides free space (if available), maintenance, and utilities with the following guidelines:

- All are set up as individual, not-for-profit corporations under the umbrella of ESDCC.
- Each reflects the work schedule of parents. (Several are also open weekends to accommodate parents' schedules.)
- Each must have its own board of directors.
- Parent fees are required but vary, depending on the determination of each individual board. Fees are on a sliding scale based on family income.
- Priority is given to state employees.
- Most centers take children from eight weeks to five years old. (There are long waiting lists for infants.) Increasingly, the centers are providing care for school-age children.

The model for the state's center, Children's Place in Albany, was established through a grant from the New York State Assembly. The center opened in 1979 with more than 100 children. There is now another center in downtown Albany, serving the children of 11,000 employees.

Many of the centers throughout the state are at psychiatric hospitals. Each hospital has between 1,100 and 2,000 employees.

New York State Psychiatric Center and State University of New York (SUNY), Binghamton, New York. There are approximately 1,200 employees of New York State in the Binghamton area. Kid Korral provides care for about 40 children aged 8 weeks to 5 years old. Tuition, which is on a sliding scale based on income, ranges between $51 and $76 per week. Hours are from 6:30 A.M. to 5:30 P.M. Monday through Friday. A catered hot lunch and two snacks are served each day. The center is closed six days a year, on government holidays.

Summer, after-school, and holiday care are also available for about 15 children 6 to 12 years old. The summer program has hours between 8 A.M. and 4:30 P.M. with fees ranging from $51 to $61 per week, or between $11.20 and $13.20 per day. Vacation holiday care for school-age children ranges between $11.20 and $16.20 per day. Begun in 1982, the center was one of the first in New York State. Renovation of the house in which the center is located cost about $30,000. About half of the children's parents are state employees, and half are county employees.

Illinois Department of Revenue, Springfield, Illinois. Opened in February 1986, the center is a new facility with over 2,100 square feet. It cares for 52 children ages two to five years old, whose parents are employed by the state. Preference is given to Department of Revenue families.

The center was developed as a nonprofit corporation through a contract between the Illinois state Department of Revenue and the Lincoln Land Community College. The latter operates the program. Fees are on a sliding scale based on income, and range between $54 per week for older children and $62 per week for younger children. Both the Department of Revenue and the Community College provide in-kind services amounting to about 35 percent of the costs. The Child Care Food Program makes up another 5 percent; parents pay about 60 percent.

In Sacramento, California, the Department of Motor Vehicles set up a center in 1975 with a loan of $20,000 from state employees and additional monies raised by parents. The center was initiated by the Commission on the Status of Women, which selected this department because of its heavy concentration of female employees. The center provides care for up to 50 children, including 15 kindergartners. Hours are from 6 A.M. to 6 P.M. and parent fees are $195 per month. According to the Department of Motor Vehicles, the center has reduced absenteeism and turnover and has helped in recruitment efforts.[16]

The Departments of Justice and Transportation in Sacramento also have programs, the former a before- and after-school program in conjunction with a nearby public school, the latter a center in a modular unit that was part of a renovation project.

City Government. Baltimore, Boston, Minneapolis, St. Louis, Newark, San Francisco, Dallas, and New York are among a growing number of cities actively involved in creating services for employees. They have been instrumental in providing the impetus for developing consortium programs.

Local Government. Some counties have innovative child care programs. Montgomery County, Maryland, bought portable buildings to provide subsidized child care adjacent to a hospital.[17]

Government involvement in child care programs has been substantial, but a recent study by Dana Friedman of the Conference Board pointed out that government emphasis on providing onetime start-up costs rather than on ongoing support to help parents (especially low-income families) pay the high costs of child care is of limited value. On the other hand, "Most exciting about the roles [government] play[s] in executing...strategies is that it involve[s] ...new forms of collaboration with the voluntary and private sectors."[18]

Centers Sponsored by Unions

The Amalgamated Clothing and Textile Workers Union (ACTWU) has pioneered the establishment of union-run child care centers. In 1966, the ACTWU negotiated an agreement with manufacturers in five states to provide child care services for children of union members. The first center was opened in 1968. The centers were funded through joint employer/union funds. Employers contributed 2 percent of their gross pay to a health and welfare fund (which was tax deductible). A joint labor/management committee administered the fund for child care and other services. The contribution accounted for about two-thirds of the operating costs, while the remainder was covered by parent fees and money from the Child Care Food Program.[19] In recent years, as the membership "aged" and issues such as job security took priority, the demand for child care decreased. The centers were closed. Diana DePugh, assistant director of Social Services, reported in 1987 that interest in child care is again surfacing in different parts of the country. The union, however, now sees itself working on child care with community agencies so that everyone—not just union members—can benefit.

A State Labor-Management Child Care Committee was established by collective agreements between state employees—members of the California State Employees' Association (CSEA), Communications Workers of America (CWA) and the California Association of Professional Scientists (CAPS)—and the state of California. The committee helps state employees develop child care programs. A Child Care Revolving Fund of $1 million provides capital for the program.[20]

It is not unusual to find centers that are collaborative efforts of union and management. Greico Brothers, which manufactures men's clothing in Lawrence, Massachusetts, provided the space and renovations for a child care center, while the Amalgamated Clothing and Textile Workers' Union pledged one penny per hour from workers' pay for one year, amounting to $12,000. In addition, the state provided a loan of $35,000 and the city a $10,000 block grant for the 48-child center.

Garment Industry, New York, New York. The International Ladies Garment Workers Union (ILGWU) provided the impetus to create a child care center for union employees in lower Manhattan. The union raised the issue to a group of manufacturers and did a study that described the need. The manufacturers then set up a nonprofit corporation to run the center, which opened in 1983. During its first two years, the center received monthly $10 contributions from several hundred small businesses. Fund-raising made up the difference, for a total of $115,000. More recently, the amounts that association members contribute have been reduced, and monies have been obtained through periodic fundraiser dinners.

The current budget for the center, which serves 85 children three to five years old, is about $400,000. The union contributes staff time and over $10,000. The New York City Agency for Child Development (ACD) provides additional funding of approximately $35 per child per week. Parents pay on a sliding scale based on income, to a maximum of $55 per week. Hours of operation are from 8 A.M. to 6 P.M.

According to Susan Cowell, executive assistant to the president of ILGWU, the center is very successful. There is low turnover among staff, in part because of the competitive salaries. The center is community based, which is especially appropriate because employees using the center live and work in the community. Liability insurance is provided through the center's association with the ACD.

Centers Sponsored by International Agencies

United Nations Day Care Center.   For over 20 years, there have been periodic attempts to establish a child care center for United Nations (UN) employees in New York City. In 1983, a UN task force contracted with the N.Y. Day Care Council to conduct a needs assessment. The assessment revealed a great need for infant care among UN employees. The task force considered starting a center on its own, but decided to ask International Preschool, a private, nonprofit corporation that operates six child care programs in Manhattan, to run the center.

A pilot program for 20 infants was begun on a part-time basis. In October 1983, the UN Day Care Center was opened in a building of the UN Development Corporation. International Preschool donates its management/ administration to the program. This includes personnel management, training, financial management, and so on. The United Nations donates space, pays utilities, and gave a one-time grant for start-up renovations and equipment.

The program serves children of UN employees from missions, agencies, or affiliates. There is an active parent education program, including periodic "brown bag" programs. Fifty-one children (six months to five years old) are enrolled. Parents pay $580 for four weeks, or $145 per week. Hours are 8:30 A.M. to 6 P.M.

Child Care Centers in Hospitals

There are currently over 500 hospitals offering child care services to their employees. The number of new programs is increasing rapidly. The National Association of Hospital-Affiliated Child Care Centers was created by hospital centers to disseminate information among programs and to interested groups. Hospitals often turn to child care for a competitive edge in recruiting nurses. According to the American Hospital Association, there is a serious and growing nursing shortage in U.S. hospitals. In 1985, the vacancy rate for registered nurses in hospitals was 6.34 percent. In 1986, it was 13.6 percent—a more than twofold increase.[21]

In addition, conventional sources of child care are usually unavailable during the hours (evenings, nights, and weekends) that nurses must work. High nurse turnover and absenteeism in many hospitals have been linked to the problems that nurses have in obtaining adequate child care. More and more hospitals are realizing that providing child care can be much less expensive than recruiting and training new nurses.

According to a 1978 study, child care centers supported by hospitals tend to have more extensive hours than other child care centers.[22] The larger hospital centers serving 100 or more children are associated with large institutions or several employers. Drawing from an extensive employee base of at least several thousand, these centers can offer seven-day-a-week care. Although these large centers may be open as late as midnight and offer care on weekends, few provide nighttime care. Many have found that few parents avail themselves of this service, preferring instead to have their children sleep at home.

Hospital-supported centers frequently charge lower fees to parent-employees than do community programs. Such centers are able to set a fee scale to attract employees to the shifts that are hard to staff. For example, Memorial Child Care Center in Long Beach, California, which is open 24 hours a day, 7 days a week, charges 50 percent less to employees using the evening and weekend shift, and provides nighttime care free of charge.

In many cases, the child care center is established as a division within the hospital. In this way, all the services of the hospital, from accounting to maintenance, are utilized. The hospital's board of directors is also the board of directors for the child care center. Employees of the child care center are on the hospital payroll and receive hospital benefits. This enables the center to attract better-trained employees.

A center can also be set up as a separate corporation, either for- or nonprofit. It can be operated by an outside agency, such as a YMCA, child care chain, or independent operator. The hospital may provide the space or start-up monies, and may receive a reduced fee per child or some other advantage. Hospitals that do not directly control their center's quality must carefully monitor the operations of the center. Where costs are kept low by paying staff the minimum wage, providing virtually no benefits, keeping the ratio of children to adults high, and laying off staff when attendance falls below established numbers for groups, the quality of care suffers.

Similarly, a "drop-in" service—which children attend on an irregular basis—can be disruptive and interfere with quality. Such a service must be carefully planned and managed. Many centers include community children to ensure full enrollment and to supplement revenue. Usually, fees for nonemployee children are higher than for employee children.

Intercare Health Services, Inc., Edison, New Jersey.   The Keith Wold Johnson Child Care Center is located on the first floor of a former school building. The building was renovated by the company to house the Pediatric Rehabilitation and the Cognitive Rehabilitation departments of John F. Kennedy Medical Center (a subsidiary of Intercare) as well as the child care center. Originally in two rooms, the center has expanded into the building as the enrollment increased to its present 125. Ninety-five children are cared for at any one time.

The Medical Center, which is a 550-bed critical care facility about 20 years old, has 2,500 employees. About 70 percent are female. Also affiliated with Intercare are three senior centers, one of which is adjacent to the center.

The child care center was established in 1983 to help recruit and retain nurses and other highly skilled professionals, such as physical and occupational therapists. According to Scott Gephard, director of Robert Wood Johnson Life Style Institute and vice president of Rehabilitation Service of Intercare, the center is "very valuable." It has enabled professional employees to advance in their careers while maintaining a family. Eighty-five employee families utilize the service. Gephard believes that two-thirds of these employees would have been lost to the hospital if not for the center. Many have been with the company for more than ten years.

Children usually enter the program at about 6 weeks old on a part-time basis. By 3 months old, they are usually full-time. Many of the mothers nurse their babies. Hours are 6:15 A.M. to 6:30 P.M. and schedules conform to hospital shifts. Employees of the hospital pay a reduced fee subsidized by the hospital—for infants, $88.25 per week compared with $132 per week for community parents. Fees for babies 19 to 30 months are $81 for employee parents and $110 for community parents. Toddler fees are $71.75 for employees and $90 for community parents, and preschool fees (3½ years to 5 years) are $64.50 for employees and $77 for community parents.

The hospital subsidizes the budget by about 25 percent or $100,000.

Methodist Hospital, Arcadia, California.   The Kathy Kredle Child Care Center was established in 1957 as a department of Methodist Hospital. One hundred and seventy children are enrolled in the center, which can care for 128 children at any one time. Approximately 70 of the children are infants, while the rest are preschoolers and kindergartners. Hours are 6:30 A.M. to 6:30 P.M. with the center accommodating to the many different schedules of hospital employees. Fees are from $1.55 per hour for preschoolers (or $70 per week) to $2.05 per hour for infants (or about $92.50 per week).

The director, Lee Wallen, who has been with the center since 1979, says that while the center charges community rates, the program actually provides more enrichment than comparable centers do. For example, ratios are 1 adult to 3 infants and toddlers, and 1 adult to approximately 9 preschoolers. (California regulations are 1 adult to 4 infants and 1 adult to 12 preschoolers.) Also, the center provides hot meals and snacks. The hospital subsidy, which amounts to about 30 percent, includes many in-kind services, such as the facility itself, laundry, accounting, dietary, housekeeping, and grounds. A study commissioned by the hospital in 1985 found that 60 to 75 percent of parents using the program reported that it raised morale and enhanced their productivity by keeping them from worrying about their children. Parents also reported that because of the program they stayed on the job 22 months longer, on average, than they might have otherwise.

Centinela Hospital, Inglewood, California.   The "hospital of the 1984 Olympics," as it is billed, is a highly successful, nonprofit 403-bed skilled nursing facility." It has several innovative satellite programs, including one at the Los Angeles Airport and another at Mammoth Ski Resort.

The hospital employs approximately 1,500 people, 70 percent of whom are female. The nursing department, the largest department in the hospital, is 98 percent female.

The child care center was started in 1982 as a division of the hospital. Prior to the center's creation, the hospital was recruiting nurses from as far away as the United Kingdom, yet a study showed that 50 percent of the nurses within the immediate community were not working. Management decided that a child care center would be a cost-effective tool for recruiting.

The center serves 60 children—36 preschoolers and 24 infants ages 6 weeks to 5 years old. Hours are 6:30 A.M. to 6:30 P.M. Schedules are flexible and conform to hospital shifts. A small weekend program for school-age children is offered. Parents pay $75 per week for infants and toddlers and $55 per week for preschoolers, less than the cost of comparable community programs. This is expensive for many employee families, but registered nurses, who earn between $24,000 and $38,000, are able to afford the program.

The operating budget is about $250,000, with the hospital paying 25 percent of the direct cost budget and providing in-kind services such as food, housekeeping, linen, space, and utilities.

Under the professional guidance of the director, Lenore Schrag, the center is a model of high-quality child care. While statistics have not been kept concerning the program's impact, managers report that turnover rate has been lowered because of the center. June Williams, Employee Relations Specialist, observed that nurses using the center return to work sooner—within six weeks on the average—after having babies. Management feels that the center has attracted employees who want to work for a "caring" institution.

Mercy Hospital, Bakersfield, California.   Mercy Hospital is a 276-bed acute-care and skilled nursing facility with 1,130 employees. The child care center, which is a division of the hospital, serves 107 children of 83 hospital employees and 45 community children, infants through age 12. Forty percent of the employees who use the center are nurses. Hours are from 6:00 A.M. to 12:00 midnight, seven days a week.

Opened in 1982, the center was designed to serve only hospital employees. However, underutilization during evening, night, and weekend hours prompted the hospital to open the center to community children. Even with the additional enrollment, the center is not fully utilized during these hours.

A survey of employees using the center found that more than one-third felt the center was an important factor in their decision to work at the hospital. Well over half of the parents also reported that they talked about the center to friends and others who inquired about working at the hospital. In addition:

56 percent reported that the center made it less likely that they would quit the hospital;

64 percent reported that the center reduced their tardiness;

54 percent reported that their absenteeism was lowered; and

42 percent reported improved productivity.

Texas Medical Center, Houston, Texas.   The Texas Medical Center was created in 1945 as the governing agency for 32 medical institutions in Houston serving 30,000 students, faculty, and professionals. The Renilda Hilkemeyer Child Care Center operates as a division of the Medical Center along with such entities as the medical center library, computer service center, and security division.

The child care center is licensed for 323 children, 6 weeks through 12 years old, and serves only the children of medical center personnel. Seventy-five percent of those who use the center are nurses. One-half of the children are under 3 years old. Hours are 6:00 A.M. to midnight, 7 days a week. Two-thirds of the children attend during the day shift and one-third during the evening.

The staff of 70 includes 54 full-time caregivers. Ratios are one adult to four infants plus an infant supervisor. Full-time care is $60 per week.

The center was begun by the director of nursing at the M.D. Anderson Cancer Hospital to aid in the recruitment of nurses. The land for the center was donated by a philanthropist. Six of the medical center institutions contribute funds directly to the child care center. The amount they contribute in any one year depends on the deficit for that year. Typically, this is about one-fifth of the total budget. The advisory board of the center consists of representatives from the contributing institutions and parents.

University Child Care Centers

Campus child care became a critical issue in the late 1960s as the demand from female students grew. Currently, the majority of all college students are women[23] and about two-thirds of all students over the age of 25 (11 million) are women.[24] Older students now make up more than one-quarter of the total, up from about 15 percent in 1965.[25]

Undergraduate as well as graduate and professional schools provide child care. The William Mitchell College of Law in St. Paul, Minnesota, has a child care center that has been in operation for more than five years. Serving 15 children of faculty, students, and the community, the center charges $2.50 per hour for infants and $2.25 for preschoolers.[26]

Approximately 40 percent of campuses offer child care, for a total of about 1,000 facilities.[27] The 1986 National Child Care Study conducted for the National Coalition for Campus Child Care Centers found that about one-quarter are on campuses with 16,000 or more students and over one-third are on campuses with under 6,000 students.[28] While the centers serve as many as 300 children, nearly one-half provide care for between 26 and 75. The average number of children in care is 62, up from 40 in 1978.

Overall, the children of students are given first priority for enrollment. More than 95 percent of the campus centers care for the children of students, 91 percent care for the children of faculty, and nearly three-quarters also serve community children.

About two-thirds of the centers receive 25 percent or less of their operating budgets from the university, compared with 50 percent or more in 1973. However, the universities provide many in-kind services, such as space, utilities and maintenance.

The majority of centers offer care for children for between 9 and 12 hours each day, or, on average, 40 hours a week. Many centers offer part-time care. Most programs care for children over one year old. About one-third provide care for infants, and less than 30 percent provide care for school-age children.

The vast majority of programs report to or are affiliated with a department of the university, most often Student Affairs or Student Services. The education, home economics, and early childhood departments were most frequently responsible for the center's administration. The centers are used for "observation, participation and research," especially by the psychology, nursing, elementary education and child development, and social science departments.

In addition,

centers used a variety of people to staff the programs. Nine out of ten centers used paid teaching personnel. College students were frequently used in campus child care centers in a variety of ways. Work study students were used as teachers at three-fourths of the centers, while two-thirds of the centers utilized student teachers and about 60 percent of the centers included student volunteers from academic classes as part of the teaching class.[29]

The University of Milwaukee Wisconsin Day Care Center. The center serves a campus population of approximately 36,000 students and 4,000 faculty and staff. Alumni and community families are also able to enroll their children in the center, as space allows.

Set up as part of the education department of the university, the center's building and grounds are provided by the university. Additional in-kind services include utilities and maintenance. Parents who are students receive tuition aid for the children from the student association.

The center operates from 6:30 A.M. to 5:30 P.M. One hundred fifty-nine children can attend at any one time. With the many part-time schedules, 280 children are enrolled. The children's schedules are based on the class schedules of their parents.

Children must be enrolled on a regular basis for at least eight hours per week, for two four-hour sessions. Enrollment is open to children from three months to six years old, and to school-age children who need care before or after school.

Nine group teachers act as "mini-directors," hiring and training teachers and developing the curricula for their groups. Because of the large number of part-time teachers, the ratio of adults to children is unusually high. Parent fees range from $99 per week for infants to $57 per week for older children. About 75 percent of the slots are used by students who are parents.

The University of California at Long Beach. The university enrolls 38,000 students. The Isabel Patterson Child Care Center serves 114 children, including 22 infants. The center is part of the School of Education and receives the space from the university. A private donor provided start-up capital for the state-of-the-art facility. The center operates between 7:00 A.M. and 6:30 P.M., Monday through Friday. Holidays correspond to those of the university; however, the program is open all summer. Scheduling is flexible, with a minimum of two hours per day, two days per week for older children, and four hours, two days per week for infants. "Drop-in" care is not provided.

Students are paid to work in the program. There are 12 full-time and 25 part-time teachers. The ratios of adults to children are: 1:3 or 1:4 for infants, 1:7 or 1:8 for preschoolers, and 1:10 for kindergartners through third graders.

Parent fees are figured on a sliding scale based on income. Generally, parents pay $1.50 per hour or $55 per week. About 80 percent of the parents are students, faculty, or staff of the university; 20 percent are from the community.

The program receives funding from the State Education Department and the student association. The amount of state funding depends on the number of low-income families using the center.

University of Madison, Wisconsin. Bernie's Place is one of several child care centers serving students, faculty, and staff of the university. Approximately 40,000 students attend the university. Forty-five children, ages 2½ to 6 years old, are cared for by the center. Approximately 75 percent of the children are from student families. Priority is given to students, faculty, and staff of the university, but community children are also served.

The center is a separate, nonprofit corporation sponsored by the Wisconsin Union Directory, a registered student organization. The university provides the building—a three-story house—plus maintenance, valued at $20,000 per year. The student union contributes approximately $3,000 per year. Parents pay $71 per week, which is slightly higher than community fees. Hours of operation are 7:00 A.M. to 5:45 P.M. with many families opting for part-time care.

Columbia University, New York, New York. Tompkins Hall Nursery School is one of three child care centers that serve the university and surrounding community. While Red Balloon and Greenhouse are full-day programs, Tompkins Hall provides nursery school—9:00 A.M. to 12:30 P.M. for three-year-olds, and 9:00 A.M. to 2:30 P.M. for four-year-olds, from September to the end of May (to conform to the regular university calendar). The school offers parents membership in the coop, which enables them to pay lower tuition. For example, five mornings cost $1,500 a year if parents belong to the coop and $2,300 if they do not.

Parents who belong to the coop either work at the school one morning a week or help out by performing a job for the school. According to Cynthia Pollack, director, "Fathers as well as mothers are active in the coop."

The program suits the needs of parents who are students and faculty at Columbia, since many have part-time schedules. Currently, slightly more than half of the 24 children have parents who are on the faculty; in past years, the majority of positions were filled by graduate students' children. About 20 percent of the children are from the community.

The school has a strong international program, with children from Israel, Pakistan, India, Japan, South Africa, Australia, and Argentina. The university provides rent, maintenance, and a subsidy that varies depending on the specific needs of the program.

Developers and Child Care

According to Albert I. Berger, senior vice-president of Helmsley-Spear, "We have been introducing child care centers into new office parks as a much-needed service. Our surveys have shown that it is the most desired amenity after food."[30]

Developers, such as Trammel Crow, Rouse and Associates, Hamilton and Associates, and Hartz are adding child care centers to business developments. Many developers who are including child care centers in office parks report that they attract tenants and provide positive community relations. A survey of 100 high-tech firms conducted by Reimer Associates, an engineering and planning firm, found that child care "ranked fourth in company relocation priorities." When child care is available, it is easier to relocate highly valued employees. Typically, the cost of building the center is absorbed by the developer while an outside agency operates the center.[31]

Municipalities, counties, and state governments are encouraging and, in some cases, mandating that developers help fund child care. San Francisco enacted an ordinance requiring developers of projects over 50,000 square feet to provide a child care center or monies to a child care fund. Likewise, Concord, California imposed a tax on developments that goes toward a child care fund (see Chapter 2).

Hacienda Business Park, Pleasanton, California. The center serves 200 children from infancy through age five whose parents are employed at AT&T Communications, Viacom Cable Television, General Electric Credit Corporation, and other corporations in the office park. Developed by Prudential Insurance Company of America and Callahan, Sweeney & O'Brian at a cost of $3.1 million (including land, building, and start-up expenses), care costs between $275 and $365 per month, lower than community rates.[32]

Trammel Crow: Dallas, Texas; Los Angeles, California; Bloomington, Minnesota. The developer Trammel Crow has developed child care centers in its office parks. A survey of the Minnesota park found that CEOs had requested it. Trammel Crow subsidizes the center.[33]

Tysons Corner, Virginia.   Money was raised by 14 companies in this Northern Virginia Business area to start a child care center for employees. Rouse and Associates, a developer, will provide the construction.

Harmon Meadow, New Jersey.   The Ministries of the Hackensack Meadowlands initiated the idea of developing the Harmony Child Care Center in an office and residential complex developed by Hartz Mountain. The $2 million center, which opened in November 1987, will serve 100 children ages 6 weeks to 6 years. Fees are $90 per week for kindergartners on up to $135 per week for infants 6 weeks to 18 months. Companies in the complex and surrounding area provided start-up monies for the project.

Consortium Centers

A consortium child care center can be formed by several employers who want to share resources, liability, and costs. Because two-thirds of all employees work in small business, there is great potential for this option.[34]

A consortium can be developed by employers in the same industry or the same geographic area. An advantage of a consortium is that the center will more likely operate at full capacity even though the needs of employees at individual companies change as children grow up. One possible drawback: companies may not want to join with other companies if they are all competing for the same employee population. Also, as Elizabeth Morgan and Diane Spearly point out, employers must be in tune philosophically and able to co-operate in planning and operating a program. Morgan and Spearly identified the following prerequisites for gaining cooperation among members of a consortium:

1. After a proposal...has been initiated, stew time must be allowed for the potential members to consider how great is their commitment.

2. Project planners are responsible for the structure and productivity of this time period.

3. Project planners can provide information on the general benefits of employer-supported child care and those specific to consortium ventures.

4. Probable costs and potential problems...and consortium participation should be discussed during stew time.

5. Most company officials will need to be educated about the requirements for quality child care.

6. [Project planners should] assist participants in clarifying both individual agency and joint consortium goals and...point out contradictory or conflicting goals.

7. A heavy requirement for financial and contractual commitment encourages prospective members to determine whether or not the costs to their individual agencies are outweighed by the benefits expected from consortium participation.

8. The sense of ownership for the project must be examined since it is a reflection of commitment to the project.

9. Cooperation...is influenced by the shared history of the participants; a history of competition can adversely affect the ability of participants to work together.[35]

Some consortia have been established in geographically defined areas, such as downtown Baltimore. The Children's Center in Baltimore was created by a joint effort of city government and private businesses. In 1978, the city council became concerned about the child care needs of the 147,000 employees in the area (40 percent of whom were women). Thirteen local employers cooperated with the council in conducting an assessment of their own employees. The results pointed to high interest in a child care center. A site, which needed some renovation, was selected, and start-up monies ($120,000) were raised through employers' contributions.

The center, a private nonprofit corporation, opened in September 1983. It provides care for 75 preschool children and can expand to serve 90 children two and a half to six years old. The hours of care are from 7:30 A.M. to 5:30 P.M., five days a week. Parents pay $365 per month. Sponsoring employers have a seat on the center's board of directors. The fact that there are plans to add new centers underscores the success of the program.

Children's Village in Philadelphia is an example of a consortium center that was established to provide work-site child care primarily for the children of employees of a particular industry—in this case, the garment industry. The center was established in 1976 by the Council for Labor and Industry. The center charges fees on a sliding scale (from $6 to $42 per week), is open 12 months a year from 7:30 A.M. to 6:30 P.M., and serves 125 children. Seventy-five percent are the children of garment workers (with 40 firms represented), and 25 percent are children of employees of nearby nongarment firms, including a hospital. The cost per child per year is $3,716, approximately 20 percent of which is paid by parents. Most of the cost is borne by the employers, the union, and the U.S. Department of Labor.

Initiated by a group of workers, the Broadcasters' Child Development Center in Washington, D.C. opened in January 1980. The board, made up of parents and representatives of seven TV and radio stations, was able to get low-interest loans (which were eventually forgiven) along with the contribution of some services from the stations. The center originally served about 50 children of parents in the broadcast industry and the community.

Located in an underutilized school building, the center was uprooted when the school district reclaimed the space for additional public school classes. It was relocated in the federal General Services Administration (GSA) headquarters, renamed the Learning Center, and designed as a demonstration project for federal agencies interested in child care. It will be expanded to serve 59 children ages three months to five years old. The fees charged are $500 per month for infants, $400 per month for toddlers, and $380 per month for preschoolers. The federal government subsidizes the program by 10 percent.

Prospect Hill Parent's and Children's Center serves employees of corporations within an office park in Waltham, Massachusetts. The center, a nonprofit corporation, was begun in 1985, the brainchild of three small corporations. Housed in a renovated facility, the center serves 45 children ages eight weeks to five years old. Parent fees are $175 for infants and $155 for toddlers, per week. Other services are provided, including resource and referral, seminars, a library, and referral for school-age care. Unfortunately, the high fees which make for a fiscally sound program also make the center prohibitive for nonsubsidized families.[36]

Sick Child Care

Sick child care is a major problem facing working parents and their employers. In 1986, the St. Paul Chamber of Commerce Child Care Task Force summarized more than 15 surveys conducted with businesses in St. Paul and Minneapolis, Minnesota. The following were their findings:

1. A sick child is the most difficult child care problem that working parents face.
2. The overwhelming majority of employees must change their child care arrangements when their children become ill. Only 8 to 19 percent of current child care arrangements were reported adequate to care for sick children.
3. The person most likely to care for the sick child is a parent, who must miss work to do so.
4. Work missed because of a sick child is a significant cause of absenteeism.[37]

National statistics show that infants have on the average seven or eight infections a year, and preschoolers six to seven.[38] As a result, absenteeism of parents can be more than ten days per year. One study found parents averaging about four and a half days per year. Another found that about one-quarter of respondents were absent an average of eight days per year because of a sick child.[39] A study in March 1984 of 5,000 employees of five large midwest companies by John Fernandez found that parents of children under 2 were far more likely to stay home when a child was sick than parents of children over 2. Sixty-one percent of mothers with children under 2 stayed home, compared to 20 percent of mothers with sick children 15 to 18.[40]

When their children are ill, between 40 percent and 50 percent of all parents stay home.[41] Other studies have found that parents who come to work when their children are sick frequently feel stress and are less productive.[42]

The problem of sick child care is not a simple one. Many parents prefer to say home with a sick child at the very beginning of an illness or if the child is very ill. When parents were asked to choose among ten employer support options, the number one choice of women with children under 13 was paid time off to care for a sick child. This same choice was the second for men with children under 13.[43]

Indeed, many businesses do allow employees to take time off to care for sick children. The St. Paul survey found that responding businesses provided employees with time off as follows:

88 percent allow employees to use unpaid absences;

86 percent allow employees to use paid personal vacation days;

58 percent allow employees to use paid personal sick days;

52 percent allow employees to use holidays;

32 percent allow employees to use other paid absences; and

43 percent provide other forms of time off, primarily by being flexible with work hours and by handling employee problems on a case by case basis.[44]

On the other hand, a 1985 survey of their readers, by *Working Mother Magazine*, found that of 1,100 respondents, many "paid" (in one way or another) for their absences to care for sick children.

The results show that sick children caused two-thirds of the parents to miss 1 to 5 days, and one parent out of 20 missed 11 or more days.

These absences were accounted for as follows:

The parent uses her own sick or vacation days	68 %
The parent loses pay	27 %
The parent makes up the time	12 %
The parent has an allotment of "sick days"	6 %
The parent works at home	8 %[45]

Until recently, most states did not allow mildly ill children in day care and none had explicit regulations for the care of sick children. Currently, many are promulgating new standards to deal with this issue.[46]

There are approximately 80 programs nationwide that offer care for sick children.[47] These include facilities especially designed to care for sick children, such as underutilized areas of hospitals, clinics, regular centers in which an area is designated a "sick bay," family day care homes, and in-home care providers. About 50 are centers, most of which are operated for profit.[48] Fees are generally high, ranging from $2 to $11 per hour, and in centers costs average $35 per day. Since many parents have to pay these fees in addition to their regular child care, subsidies can be very important.

The two most popular models are care in a hospital facility and in-home care. While there are some family day care homes providing sick care, they are less popular. A family day care home in Gardena, California, which was established through the cooperation of the city's Human Services Department, several community groups, local hospitals and $5,000 from the Mattel toy company, closed after 9 months. Only 20 families used the program. Set up to care for children 2 to 12 years old, the program was offered by the city to local businesses as part of their benefits packages. Costs were on a sliding scale from $.50 to $4 per hour. The program did not do as well as expected, probably because it was not well publicized and because a nearby hospital, Torrance, offers 24-hour sick care and a more comprehensive service.[49]

Besides needing rest, care of physical symptoms, and isolation from other children if contagious, sick children need emotional support. Therefore, programs and caregivers provide opportunities for children to visit before they are ill.

As in the case of other services, an employer can design a sick child care program specifically for its employee population, or the employer can donate money to a nonprofit corporation that provides care for the community. In either case there are tax benefits to the employer. Since the number of children who need sick care at any one time tends to be small, employers have found that a consortium approach is often a good one.

Supercare for Kids, Los Angeles, California

When TransAmerica surveyed its employees in 1984, it found that since parents were missing six and seven days a year because of sick children, the company was losing between $150,000 and $180,000 per year. In 1986 it provided start-up funds to the California Medical Center to renovate 1,300 to 1,500 feet of space in a facility two blocks from the company. The program is a nonprofit corporation operated by the Medical Center. It serves 15 children at a time from birth to 14 years old who have "mild illnesses, illnesses under treatment, post-hospitalization conditions and recovering injuries."[50] Hours are from 7 A.M. to 6 P.M. on weekdays. Corporations must enroll in order for parents to use the program. While TransAmerica and other enrolled companies pay $35 per day, parents pay $10 for the first day and $5 for each succeeding day.

Parents preregister their children for the program. Children are screened by a doctor for serious illnesses, such as chicken pox, measles, mumps, and so on before being allowed into the program. A registered nurse provides medication if needed. Toys, games, and activities are available for children and cots for resting.[51] Meals and snacks are provided. Although use has not been high, the benefit is appreciated by employees.[52]

Rainbow Shines, North Penn Hospital, Lansdale, Pennsylvania

After a survey of community child care needs, the hospital found that sick child care was in great demand. In August 1986 the program opened to hospital employees, and in September it opened to the community. With a capacity of 16 children at a time, the program is the first to be licensed by the Pennsylvania Department of Health and Welfare. It consists of two rooms adjacent to the pediatric wing of the hospital. One room is divided into three areas for children with gastrointestinal problems, upper respiratory illnesses, or general malaise. The second room, with its own air control system, is for children with chicken pox, and is the busiest according to Paul S. Cavanaugh. Hours are from 6:30 A.M. to 6 P.M. and fees $30 per day or $4 per hour. Children six weeks and up can use the program.

A parent must call in the morning and discuss the child's symptoms over the phone with a pediatric nurse before bringing the child to the center. Upon arrival the child is given another screening before placement. The center is staffed by nurses, aides, and volunteers. The program is costly for the hospital because of the hourly cost of the professionals involved. Usage was low in the beginning—in the first month only 2 children used the program. However, after ten months, 68 children had attended, about one-quarter of whom were the children of hospital employees. Five hundred children from the community are preregistered, along with 90 who are children of hospital employees. Some 15 percent of all hospital employees have enrolled.

Trust, Minneapolis, Minnesota

The sick child care service operated by this coalition of churches was initiated in 1985 with funding from the Northwest Bank of Minneapolis. In-home caregivers are recruited by Trust and trained by the Department of Health. Care is provided for children six months or older. Parents pay a $5 registration fee and from zero to $6 per hour for care, depending on family income and the professional level of the provider.[53]

Tucson Association for Child Care, Inc., Tucson, Arizona

As a nonprofit in-home care service, the association has 25 trained caregivers who care for children throughout the greater Tucson area. Parents pay on a sliding scale based on income and ranging from $1.50 to $4.25 per hour, plus $2.00 for travel expenses.[54] Several small law and accounting firms pay $8 per hour for the service for their employees.[55]

3M Corporation, Minneapolis, Minnesota

The company funded a three-year pilot project for the care of sick children of its employees. The in-home care is provided by Child Care Services, Inc., a company developed by several hospitals in 1975. While fees for the service are $8 per hour for one child and $9.50 for two, parents pay $2 per hour for one child and $2.50 for two if their annual gross family income is under $25,000; $3 for one child and $4 for two if their incomes are between $25,000 and $40,000; and $4 per hour for one child and $5.50 for two if their incomes are $40,000 or over.

Few programs exist to accommodate children with chronic illnesses, such as diabetes or arthritis, whose parents work. Yet these children need specialized care on a regular basis. Their families may need additional support to help them deal with the physical and emotional stresses involved.

Cradles and Crayons Daycare, Kansas City, Missouri

This nonprofit center serves 30 children six weeks to six years old, 70 percent of whom have special needs or chronic illnesses. Four staff nurses monitor children as they participate in play activities with caregivers. Parents pay $100 per week for full-time care. The center is also used as "respite care," or to provide parents with some time off from caregiving.[56]

Family Day Care Network

Family day care is the name given to childcare in which, typically, a woman cares for up to 6 children in her own home. More than 5 million children are cared for in this way.[57] According to studies, this is a preferred form of child care for children between one and three years old,[58] because it offers flexibility (in location, the ages of the children cared for, and the hours of care), a home-like atmosphere, and a group experience and is lower in cost than center care. In addition, siblings can be cared for together. Since it requires relatively low start-up costs, family day care can be an effective way to provide child care services to employees living in a wide geographic area. Companies with many sites may also find this an attractive option. In some cases, employers who sponsored resource and referral have become involved in family day care networks as the need for such a service became evident.

One difficulty with family day care is that the homes are often not adequately regulated by state and local agencies. Ninety-four percent of the children in family day care are in unlicensed or unregulated situations.[59]

A major study of family day care in 1981 highlighted the importance of training caregivers to provide a rich educational experience for children.[60] Recent data from the National Association for the Education of Young Children, which analyzed current research, confirms this finding.[61]

The National Association of Family Day Care Providers was created and had its first conference in Washington, D.C., in 1983. The group offers providers technical assistance and an opportunity for networking.

Employers can help develop family day care networks by contracting with experts who hire and train providers. Start-up costs are low, since providers use their own homes. The employer can offer a loan or grant to pay for any equipment or materials that providers may need, such as cribs, rugs, or toys.

The network can be organized as a nonprofit corporation, with each provider being employed by the corporation, or the providers can be established as independent small businesses, making it easier for them to continue to operate should the company discontinue its support. In helping develop independent family day care providers, the company not only achieves its goal of providing child care for employees, but also creates jobs in the community. In areas of high unemployment, this can be especially important. An employer may be eligible for government grants and other incentives for helping people become self-sufficient, especially women who are the heads of households. In families where there is only one wage earner, the spouses who stay home with young children may be trained as family day care providers. This increases family income and raises morale on the part of all employees. In this way, the company is seen as supportive of families.

Steelcase, in Grand Rapids, Michigan, provides support and technical assistance to family day care homes in the community through an in-house resource and referral service. To be part of the Steelcase network, providers must agree to participate in at least four hours of training workshops per year.

IBM provided funds to Work/Family Directions, a nonprofit resource and referral service, to develop family day care homes. The funding goes to family day care networks located in employees' home neighborhoods to recruit and train providers.

Recognizing that family day care is usually located near employees' homes and therefore may cover a broad geographic area, many employers are taking a consortium approach to developing family day care. They are donating funds to agencies that specialize in recruiting, training, and monitoring providers. Frequently, government grants are also obtained since the networks are seen as serving the entire community.

California Resource and Referral Agency, San Francisco

This agency was created to represent and provide technical support to the 65 resource and referral agencies throughout California that are loosely connected as an association. In 1985, with monies from BankAmerica Foundation, Pacific Telesis Group, Chevron, Clorox, Mervins department stores, and many other companies and government agencies, it developed a program to recruit and train family day care providers in more than 20 cities throughout the state. The program received high praise for exceeding its goal by 20 percent during the pilot phase, recruiting and training more than 200 family day care providers (with the aid of seven community colleges) to care for 1,100 children. In 1987 the program received $1.1 million in funding, and plans to train 640 new providers to care for 3,200 children.[62]

According to the Year-End Report:

These outcomes mark a new milestone in the professionalization and development of family day care in California. By improving the self-image and enhancing the caregiving skills of new and existing providers, the initiative has promoted a public perception of family day care as a viable and acceptable child care choice.[63] (Also see Chapter 3 on resource and referral.)

The Neighborhood Child Care Initiatives Project, New York, New York

In 1986, New York City had only 80,000 licensed child care slots for 250,000 children under five. American Express Foundation initiated the project by providing $50,000 to Child Care Inc., a resource and referral agency, to create 12 family day care homes to care for approximately 60 children. The project has now received $400,000 from ten corporations, including Carnegie Corporation, Chase Manhattan, Con Edison, and Manufacturers Hanover.[64]

School-Age Child Care

School-age child care is needed any time children are not in school while their parents are working—on a daily basis, before and after school, during holidays and vacations, and especially during the summer months.

The loneliness and fear felt by latchkey children (school-age children who must be at home alone), while waiting for a parent to come home, have been documented by Lynette and Thomas Long, who interviewed more than 500 of them.[65]

Their work has been confirmed by other researchers such as Rickey L. Williams and Patricia D. Fosarelli, who analyzed calls to a children's telephone call-in service in Baltimore and Tucson. They found that the vast majority of calls were made because of loneliness or boredom. In 63 percent of the cases in which the child had a medical problem, no adult was present. The median age of callers was 9.7 years old.[66]

The number of latchkey or "self-care" children is increasing, especially among 9 to 11 year olds. Several million children spend before- and after-school hours without supervision. Often managers in corporations are aware of the "three o'clock panic" that many working parents feel, worrying whether their children have arrived home safely (see Chapter 2).

After-school care can be in the child's home, someone else's home (family day care), a child care center, a community or private agency, or a school facility. Only about 150 school districts in the United States offer after-school programs.[67] Special interest programs such as arts and crafts, dance, and sports are also school-age programs. Some parent groups have found that if they pay for a teacher, schools will remain open beyond 3 P.M. to house a program.

A 1987 study of school-age child care needs in the city of Boston, conducted by the School Age Child Care Project of the Wellesley Center for Research on Women, found only 65 center-based school-age programs "with the capacity to serve 2635 children throughout the city, representing 4% of the school-age children."[68] An especially acute situation exists in the need for subsidized school-age care for low-income families. The Department of Social Services funds 1,378 slots serving only 2 percent of school-age children in the city; 36 percent of the children qualify for public assistance.[69] Besides the need for affordable care, the study found a need to coordinate services. Since racial integration policies require many children to be bused to schools, decisions also must be made about where to develop programs—near children's homes or near the schools they attend.

School-age children can also benefit from training in self-help skills. State Mutual Life Assurance Company of America in Worchester, Massachusetts, offers a program for employees and their school-age children called, "I'm In Charge." Five two-hour sessions conducted by a Training and Development consultant and the assistant vice president of Human Resources and Media Development teach parents and children how to manage self-care. Parents are shown how to set rules and monitor children at home. Children are taught safety skills, how to solve problems that might arise, and how to care for other children while alone. The program was originally developed by the Kansas Committee on Child Abuse for use in schools.[70]

Other programs include "warm lines" or phone numbers that children can call while they are caring for themselves. Specially trained people answer questions and reassure children, helping them cope with being alone and organizing their time. In Kansas City, Missouri, a television station, KCTV, provides more than $100,000 per year for PhoneFriend. The money pays for publicity, space, telephones, office equipment, printing for the brochure, and "the all-important sticker with the warmline number on it and an actively involved staff liaison."[71] Family and Child Services of Kansas City provides $18,000 per year toward the project, which covers a part-time coordinator, phone bills, and other incidental expenses.

In cities across the country, community groups are initiating after-school programs and involving businesses in their support. Houston, Texas, has a comprehensive after-school program which is funded by local businesses and coordinated by the Houston Committee for Private Sector Initiatives. In Sioux Falls, South Dakota, Gannett Foundation provided funding for KARE-4, a cooperative effort with the YM and YWCA, and the Boys Club and Girls Club, to provide programming and transportation. Northwest Bank's Foundation in Minneapolis, Minnesota funded a joint effort with the public schools in areas where bank branches are located, to provide before- and after-school care for children.[72]

Employers have developed a variety of initiatives to respond to this need. Fel Pro provides a summer camp for employees' children. In 1970 the company purchased over 200 acres of rural property that was intended as a recreational area for employees about 40 minutes from the plant. The property was developed for children ages 7 to 15 years old. Today over 300 children attend the Triple-R camp, for which parents pay $15 per week per family. The camp costs the company $80,000 a year to operate.

The company finds that the program has a positive impact on recruitment and retention of personnel. It has also developed a child care center for young children. Other employers with existing on- or near-site child care centers catering to younger children, such as Hoffmann-LaRoche, Wang, and ISI, have found it advantageous to accommodate school-age children as well.

Dow Chemical, which is the major employer in Midland, Michigan, was concerned about public relations after having to lay off workers. Kathy McDonald, Housing Coordinator for the company, spent three years researching ways Dow could be supportive of families. The company decided to make charitable donations to the United Way to develop child care services. Dow provided $35,000 in seed money for the development of a resource and referral agency, Child Care Concepts, and $5,000 toward the creation of an out-of-school care program, Kids Club. The program, which is licensed by the Michigan Department of Social Services, is sponsored by Camp Fire, a 77-year-old nationwide youth organization. It serves children 6 to 12 years old and offers "active and quiet play including crafts, games, stories, special projects, time for school work if needed and nutritious snacks."[73] Parents pay a $10 registration fee which includes insurance and membership dues, plus $2 per hour to cover the cost of program operation.

Arylawn School-Age Program, National Institutes of Health, Bethesda, Maryland

Started in 1976 with a grant from NIH, the Netty Ottenberg Memorial Day Care Center outgrew its original space on the NIH campus and was relocated to the Arylawn building, about a block away. The program serves 170 children ages 3 to 13, 150 of whom are in kindergarten or above. Hours are from 7:30 A.M. (preschoolers and afternoon kindergartners attend in the morning) to 6:00 P.M. weekdays, and on days when public schools are closed but federal government offices are open. The program is especially appealing to parents because activities that children normally have to travel to—such as Girl Scouts or gymnastics—are arranged right at the center, along with the regular activities. Fees range from $42 to $50 per week, with scholarships available. The center offers a "camp-like" summer program for 120 children, which costs $75 per week. About 80 percent of the parents using the center are NIH employees.

Dr. Ann Schmitz, the director, reports that the program is entirely self-sufficient. However, the government provides important public relations, for example, in facilitating cooperation with the Montgomery County school board. The school district provides transportation to the program.

Other School-Age Options

An employer can contract with a local school to remain open, and either the school or the employer can hire caregivers to care for the children of employees.

Family day care providers can be trained to care for school-age children as well as younger children. In 1985, Child Care Systems, a resource and referral company in Lansdale, Pennsylvania, started such a network for school-age children in the Philadelphia area. Care is provided from 7 A.M. to 9 A.M. and 3 P.M. to 6 P.M. on school days, snow days, and school holidays. Fees are $10 per week for before-school care and $30 per week for after-school care. Providers pay a portion of their fees to Child Care Systems for monthly meetings, lending library, and so on.[74]

A child care resource and referral service can include information about programs for school-age children, such as sports programs like ice skating or swimming, since parents may want to arrange different experiences for their children during these hours.

Young adolescents also need programs before and after school. The Center for Early Adolescence reports that one option for 10- to 15-year-olds is to help in early childhood programs. However, many states prohibit this participation. Communities, such as New York City, are beginning to change the regulations, recognizing that although adolescents may be too old for regularly supervised school-age programs, they can benefit from providing a service (such as caring for young children) while themselves being supervised.[75]

The School-Age Child Care Project at the Wellesley College Center for Research on Women provides information and technical assistance about care for children aged 5 to 12 years. In recognition of its importance, the center has been funded by several foundations such as the Ford, Carnegie, and Levi Strauss foundations, among others. The Center for Early Adolescents provides information about programs for children 10 to 14 and funds research projects.

Worksheet 13
On- or Near-Site Child Care Center Regulations

This chart will help you know at a glance the minimum requirements for a child care center in your area. Contact local licensing agencies for the following information. (See Appendix A). Include regulations for specific age groups.

State for Local Licensing Agency:

Phone: Contact Person: Date:

Space Requirements

Adult/Child Ratios (by age)

Group Size

Health/Safety Standards and Procedures

Staff Educational Requirements/Credentials

Program Requirements (Developmental Curriculum, etc.)

Worksheet 14
On- or Near-Site Child Care Center Preliminary Analysis: Operating Budget

This analysis will help estimate the cost of a center. Use information from your needs assessment (see Chapter 4) to complete items 1, 2 and 8. Use information from Licensing (Worksheet 13) for items 3 and 6.

1. Approximate no. of children in the program:

6wks-18mos.____ 18mos – 3yrs.____ 3yrs. – 5 yrs.____ School-age____

2. No. of parents preferring hrs. of operation:

6a.m. – 3p.m.____ 7a.m. – 4p.m.____ 8a.m. – 5p.m.____ etc.

3. Space requirements
Square footage per child X no. of children in each age group

6wks – 18mos _____ X _____ = _____

18mos – 3 yrs. _____X _____= _____

3yrs – 5 yrs _____ X _____ =_____

School-age _____X_____ = _____

Other(including
staff room,
admin.,etc.   _____

Total   _____ X _____ = _____
                               rent/square = Yearly Cost
                                    foot   of Space

4. Materials and Equipment

No. of class____ X _____cost/class/= _____Total cost of
   rooms   year   Materials/Equip.

5. Administrative Costs

Telephone   _____
Electricity, heat, etc._____
Postage   _____
Maintenance/repairs_____
Laundry   _____
Consumables   _____

6. Insurance cost _____

7. Food/child/year _____

8. Staff
   Educational

No. of children   No. of adults needed (based on ratio)

6wks – 18mos____   _____x salary + benefits = _____staff costs

18mos – 3 yrs____ _____etc.

                                    _____Total Ed.

   Administrative
(bookkeeper, cook, etc.)   salary + benefits = _____Total Admin.

9. Approx. Operating Costs = _____

   Approx. Cost/Child/Year = _____

10. Suggested Parent Fees
Fixed (based on age of child – the younger the child, the higher the fee;
sliding scale based on income, e.g. under $10,000 _____etc.)

6wks – 18mos.$_____ 18mos – 3 yrs. $_____etc.

11. Family Income

Under $10,000_____ $10,000 – $15,000_____etc.

12. Suggested Company Subsidy

Amount per child $_____
(For DCAP see Chapter 3)

Amount of charit.
contribution $_____

In-kind services $_____

Worksheet 15
On- or Near-Site Child Care Center Preliminary Analysis: Start-Up Budget

1. Possible Sites

Location   cost of construction/ X no. of sq. ft. =   Total cost
                or renovation

_____   _____ X _____ = _____

2. Equipment and Materials

No. of classrooms_____ X cost to equip each_____= Total_____

3. Staff

Director salary/mo. _____ X no. of months_____= Total_____

4. Consultant fees

Employer-supported
child care consultant_____

Architect_____

5. Communications _____

Estimated total $_____

NOTES

1. Dawson, Mikel, Lorenz, and King, *An Experimental Study of the Effects of Employer-Sponsored Child Care Services*, pp. vii–viii.

2. Hofferth, and Phillips, "Child Care in the United States," p. 559.

3. Kathryn Senn Perry, *Survey and Analysis of Employer Day Care in the United States*, Ph.D. dissertation, University of Wisconsin, 1978.

4. Clifford Baden and Dana E. Friedman, Editors, *New Management Initiatives for Working Parents*, Boston: Wheelock College, 1981, p. 32.

5. "Worksite Child Care Centers: Experiences of Eight Workplace Centers Summarized," pp. .007.6–9.

6. Hofferth and Phillips, "Child Care in the United States," p. 567.

7. Ibid.

8. Child Care Action Alliance, "Employer-Supported Child Care—Summary of a Survey," Ardmore, Penna.: Child Care Action Alliance, Fall 1980.

9. Roupp, *Children at the Center*.

10. Perry, *Survey and Analysis of Employer Day Care*.

11. Institute for Scientific Information, "Fact Sheet," Philadelphia: Institute for Scientific Information, Inc., 1982, p. 1.

12. Resources for Child Care Management, "Child Care at the Workplace," Conference Materials, Chicago, June 11, 1987, p. 19.

13. Cathy Trost, "Child Care at Virginia Firm Boosts Worker Morale and Loyalty," *The Wall Street Journal*, February 12, 1987, p. 27.

14. Resources for Child Care Management, "Child Care at the Workplace," p. 5.

15. Resources for Child Care Management, Dana E. Friedman, speech at the conference, "Child Care at the Workplace."

16. Friedman, *Government Initiatives to Encourage Employer-Supported Child Care*, p. 74.

17. Bob Horowitz, "Day Care: A Problem That Isn't Going to Go Away," the *Montgomery Journal*, June 15, 1987, p. A9.

18. Friedman, *Government Initiatives*, p. 88.

19. U.S. Department of Labor, *Community Solutions for Child Care*, report of a Conference co-sponsored by the Women's Bureau, the National Manpower Institute, and the National Commission on Working Women, Washington, D.C.: U.S. Department of Labor, Office of the Secretary, Women's Bureau, March 1970, p. 27.

20. Lydenberg, "Child Care Update," p. 5.

21. "U.S. Hospitals Facing Shortage of Nurses," *The Journal of Commerce*, January 30, 1987.

22. Empire State Day Care Services, "On-Site Day Care: State of the Art and Models Development," report for the New York State Governor's Office of Employee Relations, February 1980, p. 20.

23. U.S. Bureau of the Census, "School Enrollment, Social and Economic Characteristics of Students; October 1985," Series P-20, No. 409, U.S. Bureau of the Census: Current Population Reports, from "Colleges Conquer the Baby Bust," *American Demographics*, September 1987, p. 31.

24. Rhoda M. Galinsky, "Day Care Finds a Home on Campus," *New York Times*, January 8, 1984, p. 14.

25. U.S. Bureau of the Census, "Colleges Conquer Baby Bust," p. 31.

26. "Legal Child Care," *ABA Journal*, June 1, 1987, p. 23.

27. Nancy Day, "Day Care Comes to the Campus," *Working Mother*, January 1984, pp. 37–41.

28. Herr, Zimmermann, and Saienga, *The National Child Care Study*.

29. Ibid., p. 96.

30. Albert Bergen, "Readers Report—Child Care Centers Are Blossoming in Office Parks," *Business Week*, June 29, 1987, p. 6.

31. California Resource and Referral Network, "A Developer's Guide to Child Care," p. 5.

32. Cathy Trost, "Toddling Trend: Child Care Near the Office," *The Wall Street Journal*, October 6, 1986, p. 33.

33. Ibid.

34. Baden and Friedman, *New Management Initiatives*, p. 47.

35. Morgan and Spearly, *Child Care Consortiums by Employers*, p. 11.

36. "Child Care at the Workplace," Conference materials, p. 2.

37. St. Paul Chamber of Commerce Child Care Task Force, "The Sick Child Care Dilemma," p. 2.

38. Paul S. Cavanaugh, North Penn Hospital, "Workplace Child Care: Benefits and Services," Speech given at U.S. Department of Labor Women's Bureau Conference, Philadelphia, June 25, 1987.

39. Ibid., p. 3.

40. Ibid., p. 5.

41. Ibid., p. 3.

42. John Fernandez, quoted in "Corporate Support Gives Boost to Services That Care for Working Parents' Sick Kids," by Joann S. Lublin, *Wall Street Journal*, November 18, 1986, p. 35.

43. Ibid., p. 4.

44. St. Paul Chamber of Commerce Child Care Task Force, "The Sick Child Care Dilemma," p. 2.

45. Ibid., p. 6.

46. Fredericks, Hardman, Morgan, and Rodgers, *A Little Bit Under the Weather*, pp. 20–23.

47. Lublin, "Corporate Support," p. 35.

48. Elder, "New Focus on Day Care," p. 1.

49. "Sick Care in Home Project Flops," *Day Care U.S.A.*, Vol. 16, No. 6, March 2, 1987, p. 1.

50. "Supercare for Kids" Brochure, California Medical Center, Los Angeles, California.

51. "Day Care for Sick Children Helps Hold Down Costs," *Personnel Management and Compensation*, Vol. 6, No. 9, September 10, 1986, p. 7.

52. Allan Halcrow, "A New Twist on Child Care," *Personnel Journal*, November 1986, pp. 8, 11.

53. Fredericks, Hardman, Morgan, and Rodgers, *A Little Bit Under the Weather*, p. 63.

54. Ibid., p. 42.

55. Chapman, "Executive Guilt," p. 35.

56. Jilian Mincer, "Day Care Center for Sick Children," *New York Times*, July 2, 1987, p. C9.

57. Patricia Divine-Hawkins, *National Day Care Home Study Final Report*, pp. 2–3.

58. Ibid., p. 3.

59. Ibid., p. 5.

60. Ibid., p. 35.

61. Deborah Phillips, *Quality in Child Care.*

62. Joan O'C. Hamilton, "California Makes Business a Partner in Child Care," *Business Week*, June 8, 1987, p. 100.

63. Lawrence, *California Child Care Initiative Year-End Report*, p. 3.

64. Nancy Kolben, "Does the Big Apple Shine? NYC Supports for Working Parents," *Business Link*, Summer 1986, p. 13.

65. Long and Long, *The Handbook for Latchkey Children and Their Parents*, p. 12.

66. School-Age Child Care Project, *Boston School-Age Child Care Coordination Project: A Progress Report*, Wellesley College Center for Research on Women, October 1987, pp. 3–4.

67. Joan M. Bergstrom and Eleanor T. Nelson, "Latchkey Kids: Corporate Solutions to the Three O'Clock Syndrome," *Employee Services Management*, March 1987, p. 13.

68. School-Age Child Care Project, *Boston School-Age Child Care Coordination Project*, p. 10.

69. Ibid., pp. 11–12.

70. Allan Halcrow, "Child Care: The Latchkey Option," *Personnel Journal*, July 1986, pp. 12–13.

71. "KCTV Is 'On the Line' for School-Age Children in Kansas City," *Business Link*, Vol. 2, No. 2, Summer 1986, p. 9.

72. Bergstrom and Nelson, "Latchkey Kids," p. 13.

73. Kids Club, "What a Way to Grow," brochure.

74. "Home Providers For Latch-Key Kids Only." *Day Care USA*, Vol. 15, No. 22, June 13, 1986, p. 2.

75. "Rules Hamper Young Adolescent Programs, Book Says," *Day Care USA*, Vol. 16, No. 9, April 1987, pp. 3–4.

5

GETTING THE JOB DONE

GATHERING INFORMATION, MAKING DECISIONS, AND PLANNING THE PROGRAM

To plan the right program for working parents, four factors must be taken into consideration: (A) range of options; (B) employer perspective/management goals; (C) parents' needs; and (D) community resources. Together these factors provide a framework for successful decision making.

Someone within Personnel may be assigned the task of studying the issue of child care and making recommendations, or a task force or committee, representing all company constituencies, may be charged with the responsibility of gathering information. Whoever takes responsibility for the issue will need to be knowledgeable about the way in which the company makes decisions; for example, what kind of information is needed, how it should be presented, and so forth. You will need hard facts. Become familiar with parents' needs, the child care system, and the range of options, and select a reputable consultant to help you.

If a task force has been created to look into the issue of child care, the varied expertise of the members can be put to use. Personnel specialists can provide information about trends in hiring; an employee relations expert can offer insight into employees' points of view; a financial expert can help in analyzing costs; a computer expert can help in organizing and summarizing the data from the questionnaire.

There are several reasons for including a number of people in the general thinking and planning from the beginning: to assess company atmosphere and the positive and negative aspects associated with taking this kind of step; to educate and bring people from all levels of the organization along as plans proceed, and help them feel involved in the process; and to develop a shared understanding of how programs will fit in with current corporate philosophy and future plans.[1]

Research by Dana Friedman of the Conference Board found that members of task forces frequently included representatives from:

- Human resources (benefits, personnel, employee counseling program, medical, corporate recruiter)
- Community affairs
- Public affairs
- Government affairs
- Training and development
- Corporate research
- Corporate librarian
- Legal counsel
- Corporate treasurer
- Labor relations[2]

The task force should be large enough to handle all the work but not so large that discussion becomes unwieldy. The Conference Board study found that task forces usually numbered between 6 and 20 members. However, the smaller groups were more effective.[3]

Many corporations are adopting Japanese-style "quality circles" that are groups of employees who help solve company-wide problems. When employees are involved in this way their understanding of the complexity of an issue is increased and they are more likely to support the action their company takes.

Some companies, such as Northwest Bank, have open membership to the task force—anyone who wants to can serve. There is a selective process involved to assure a balance of representation from throughout the company.[4] The point is that by encouraging interested employees to take part in the process, more actual work gets done.

In a study that the author conducted, several employees came forth who had backgrounds in early childhood education and had cared for children. They were eager to help in the planning and their input was very useful. In order to get a variety of perspectives and interests, be sure to also encourage employees who do not have children to participate.

Knowing the Range of Child Care Options

Familiarize yourself with already existing employer-supported programs in your community. If none exist, look at communities nearby or companies similar to yours for examples. Business organizations, such as the Chamber of Commerce, professional associations, such as the American Association of Personnel Administrators, and women's organizations, such as the Financial Women's Association, can help you identify resources and stimulate interest in the issue by conducting conferences. Government organizations, such as the Women's Bureau, or individuals, such as the mayor, are also important sources of information (see Worksheet 16).

Selecting a Consultant

For effective decision making, you will need in-depth information. A professional in employer-supported child care can guide you through the process, providing the specific information and perspective you need at each stage. The right consultant will know what other employers have done and are doing, what the child care provider system is like in your community, and, in a general sense, what parents' needs and preferences are. The consultant should also help you identify the specific needs of your employees and understand how these needs can be met within the context of your company's benefit plans and policies. In working with a company liaison or task force, the consultant must maintain confidentiality.

Professional consultants charge between $200 and $1,000 per day. You should budget between $10,000 and $20,000 for professional help in conducting an entire study, depending on the size of the company, the number of sites, and so on.

An in-depth feasibility study should take several months. Without professional help, the time required and the real cost are actually higher, since employees (who are paid to do other jobs) must spend many hours collecting data that are not readily available to people unfamiliar with the field. One human resource professional spent several weeks contacting local child care providers for information. Because he did not know what questions to ask, he received an enormous amount of information that he was not able to organize easily, a task that could have been done fairly quickly by an expert in employer-supported child care.

One high-tech company assigned the task to a group of computer programmers. They spent so many hours compiling lists of child care services that by the time the lists were complete, they were out of date.

Company Perspective/Management Goals

Why Management Is Interested

If you know why top management is interested in the needs of working parents, you can tailor your approach to achieve optimum impact. There are several reasons why management may be interested: personnel strategies, public relations/corporate image, keeping up with competitors, and personal or social goals of administrators.

Personnel Strategies.   Many employers are beginning to be concerned about the future availability of certain groups of employees. One reason is that the numbers of highly skilled professionals and entry-level employees are decreasing and will continue to decrease throughout the 1990s, according to demographers such as Herbert Bienstock.[5] Many employers believe that offering some form of child care support will give them an edge in recruiting skilled employees in industries such as health care and high technology, where women are an increasingly important segment of the work force.

A high-tech corporation on Long Island began a study of the child care needs of employees when managers noted that the percentage of females hired during the last three years had more than tripled. The company doctor reported that many young women had expressed concern about quality child care. One highly valued worker, who left the company after having a baby, wrote to her superior, "I just could not find the kind of care I could feel comfortable about. I think that if you helped employees find this, you would keep them."

A hospital administrator remarked that he was most concerned about retaining excellent staff. The hospital's child care center enabled women to return to work after having their babies. The administrator noted that during a particularly difficult nursing shortage his hospital was able to keep its full-time staff and a large pool of part-time nurses—a group notably difficult to retain—by accommodating to their child care needs.

Many corporations are aware that child care problems can cause absenteeism. An obvious example is when a child or a caregiver is sick and there is no one to care for the child, or a caregiver quits with no notice. Less obvious is the effect on productivity when working parents are not happy with their child care arrangements.

The personnel director of a large manufacturing plant noticed that many of the secretaries seemed to work less efficiently as the hour approached 3 P.M. On closer examination, he discovered that mothers throughout the office began calling home at about that time to see if their young school-age children had arrived home safely. He found that no provisions had been made by the community schools to supervise these children after the school day ended. He was instrumental in beginning an after-school program in the community.

Public Relations/Corporate Image.   A company's product or service may be family- or child-related. Such a company may decide that it is in its own best interest to support working parents—not just its own employees but others in the community as well. Stride Rite, which makes children's shoes, created a child care center in Boston for employee and community children. Steelcase, a family-run business, has an information and referral service that provides training for family day care providers and child care centers throughout the community of Grand Rapids, Michigan. Corning Glass Foundation provided start-up and ongoing support for a center that serves its community in Corning, New York. Since community involvement was a priority, community parents were involved from the beginning in assessing the needs and planning the program.

Johnson Wax, a 100-year-old family-owned company, presents itself as innovative and supportive of the work and family needs of employees. The company has offered paid vacations and profit-sharing since the early 1900s, and has never laid off employees. The child care center, which was created in 1983, followed development of a wellness program.

The public relations benefits of company involvement in child care can be realized in a variety of ways. Many companies have representatives conduct workshops and speak at conferences about their child care programs. Most have lively brochures and literature. Some, such as Corning, have created slide shows that can be borrowed and shown throughout the country. In Corning's slide presentation, the president and other executives are presented as caring individuals, committed to the welfare of the community.

Keeping up with Competitors.   While most companies do not want to be the first in their community to offer a new program, they also do not want to be the last. If you have been assigned the task of looking into child care issues because your company is concerned about what competitors are doing, you will probably focus your study on other firms in your industry, paying special attention to those nearby. However, it is important that you do not simply imitate a competitor's program. Just because a program exists does not mean it is worthwhile or cost-effective. Knowing what competitors are doing, or planning to do, is an important first step in your investigation. However, since each situation is unique, you must be aware of all the options in order to create a program specific to the goals and needs of your own company.

Personal/Social Goals of Administrators.   Who initiated the study of child care is important. If the impetus came from the president, you are assured of major support within the organization. If it came from employees, however, management may be highly skeptical. Your recommendations will have to overcome resistance on the part of those who may not be personally concerned with child care.

A top executive with a personal conviction about child care support for working parents may have initiated the investigation. Talk with this person. Find out what options he or she is especially interested in. The executive may have in mind a specific type of program, such as support for children with special needs or summer care for school-age children.

Format for Obtaining and Presenting Information

Each company has its own preferred way of researching and presenting new ideas. You will need to get input from upper-level managers to shape an optimally effective study. In some companies, such studies may result in a short letter to the president, stating basic facts about the issue and making general recommendations. In other companies, a more lengthy report, including extensive background information, is presented to upper management, or a formal proposal is made, documenting the needs and offering specific recommendations. In all cases, sample budgets are essential, even if they are only rough estimates.

What Information Do You Need?

No matter how or why a study was initiated, information about what other employers are doing is important. What kinds of programs have been created, how much they cost, how they have advanced company objectives—such facts provide a frame of reference in which your company can design its own response to the needs of working parents.

You will need to describe various options for support that many people have not heard of. Not only must you describe the broad range of possibilities, but you need to know how combinations of options can be used to solve specific problems.

Where possible, include data about other kinds of company-supported programs that resemble child care support in their approach. Examples are EAPs, which help employees deal with personal problems, employee van pools or credit unions, which enlist the cooperation of employees in solving transport or financial problems, and wellness programs.

Management will want to know the tax and legal implications of the various options. An expert from the tax department should be consulted.

Parents' Needs

Employers may hesitate about involving employees in a study for fear of raising expectations for one specific service, such as a child care center or a financial subsidy for child care. Throughout this discussion, we will point out how this danger can be avoided. At this point, however, we can state with assurance that when employees become knowledgeable about the complexity of the issue—specifically, when they realize the range of other employees' needs—they are usually quite flexible in their expectations and cooperative in providing the data you need to develop services appropriate to the situation.

Informal Needs Assessment

The first step in finding out about the child care needs of employees is an informal needs assessment. Without doing a scientific study, you can get a great deal of information that will start you thinking along the lines of an appropriate response for your employees. Although an informal needs assessment does not have to involve employees directly, it is most effective when it does.

Demographic Data from Personnel Records. Your consultant in employer-supported child care can guide you in obtaining the information necessary to determine the best options for your company. Such information includes: where employees live, their salaries, how long they have been with the company, and male-to-female ratios. Your insurance company can give you data about the number of employees who make health claims for dependents. For example, if a large percentage of employees are females, were hired within the last five years, and live in suburbs near work, they may have a larger number of children. Use census data to estimate the percentages of two-career families, single parents, and so on.

Exit interviews can be useful in providing information about child care needs. The personnel department may be able to provide numbers or proportions of employees who have left because of child care related problems. It is also possible that child care problems are associated with a specific department or division of the company because of work hours, supervisory policies, overtime expectations, and so forth.

Employee Interviews, Targeted Groups.   A great deal of information can be obtained through informal conversations with individuals. The head of an Employee Assistance Program (EAP) kept hearing about child care concerns while counseling employees about other problems—marital relationships, alcoholism, financial concerns, and so on. When he tried to arrange infant care for the child of an alcoholic mother, he discovered that there were no programs in her community that covered her work hours. He reasoned that other people must be having similar problems in finding child care, and he was able to alert management to the issue.

Many corporations have forums for groups of employees to talk about personal concerns and needs. A high-tech company in California uses a technique called "sensing," in which small groups of employees meet with their superiors to air their likes, dislikes, and suggestions for changes. A large association that employs about 1,000 has an employee committee that reviews employees' suggestions and makes recommendations to management. Since child care was raised by several employees, the committee decided to recommend that the association hire a consultant to conduct a study of the needs.

Focus groups must be led by experts. The questions asked must be couched in the language of child care and parenting. Also, you must be careful that the discussion brings out the attitudes of the entire group and not just of one or two individuals. For this reason, groups must be kept small (no more than 15 people). They should also include employees who are more or less on the same job level.

Information must be kept confidential. There may be people who are reluctant to disclose certain information about themselves in a group setting. You may want to invite people to communicate with the expert privately if they so desire. On the other hand, the information obtained in this manner may provide managers with insight about employee needs that can be useful in their work. At a hospital in upstate New York, the author conducted groups in the presence of the employee ombudsman. Since her role involves advocating for employees and responding to their problems, she found the sessions extremely useful. She reported that she had not realized how hard it was for some employees to find quality child care to cover their work hours. She believes that this experience has expanded her understanding of the challenge that employees of hospitals face in managing their family needs.

You should be aware that those who volunteer for groups may not reflect the entire employee population. Try to speak with groups representing all employees, whether exempt, nonexempt, union, upper management, and so on.

While information obtained through discussion is by definition anecdotal, you will nevertheless get a sense of some of the more pressing problems encountered by employees. For example, when the author conducted targeted groups for a rural corporation she found that the majority of employees had never seen a child care center or a licensed or registered program, and had relied entirely on informal child care. Several reported having very low quality and unreliable care and experiencing constant anxiety about their arrangements. Worksheet 17 can help you select a consultant to conduct focus groups.

Workshops/Seminars. Workshops that are held to provide parents with information about child care can also serve to communicate employee needs to the employer. In the process of informing parents about such topics as "Definition of quality child care," "Types of services available for children under the age of six," and so forth, the sessions can generate data about the ages of the children, the types of care used and their costs, where people live, and other data. Information gathered in this way must be kept confidential, but summaries of the data can be used to apprise management of general needs and trends.

To stimulate discussion, the leader should ask open-ended questions, such as "What kind of care are you now using?" and "How do you feel about it?" You want to find out what kind of care people prefer, how they manage when children or caregivers are sick, and what their concerns are about child care and parenting. Be sure that all ages of children are considered. Parents of older children have different kinds of problems, but these problems may be just as pressing as those faced by parents of very young children (see Worksheet 18).

Formal Needs Assessment

The formal needs assessment is an instrument for getting specific information about large numbers of employees, usually through a written questionnaire, or, less commonly, telephone interviews.

The questionnaire should be carefully tailored to your company. As you design the survey tool, keep in mind the following:

What Information Do You Want to Obtain? When assessing child care needs, it is useful to organize your data into subcategories based on employee family types. Four groups that you will want to know about are: employees who have dependent children, employees who do not have children yet but are planning to have them within the next several years, employees who have children and intend to have more within the next several years, and employees who do not have and do not intend to have children in the near future.

You can compare these groups in terms of family data—income, proximity to work, and so on—and work data—type of job, number of years on the job, work hours, overtime, and attitudes toward employer-support for working parents. The company's decision to provide a service should take into account the opinions of those employees who will not avail themselves of the service. For example, a question that was part of a survey conducted by the author asked for opinions about whether the company *ought* to provide a service for working parents. The majority of employees without children, as well as those with children, agreed. In a section soliciting comments, several employees without children reported that their coworkers' struggles with child care affected them—they might have to cover for a parent whose child care "fell apart." Therefore, they wanted the company to support working parents.

Information should be obtained about the number and ages of children and how they are cared for. This data will enable you to determine the type of child care that employees are most comfortable with and the fees they are accustomed to pay for care. If you plan to introduce a new service—one that is not familiar to employees—you will have to plan an intensive educational campaign to enlighten them about the advantages of the service.

You can also identify patterns or trends in family structure. You may find, for example, that families are having fewer children—that those with older children tend to have larger families than those with younger children. In one study conducted for a hospital the author found that there was a fairly constant number of children of each age (by year) from 1 to 15 years old. The number of employees who were pregnant also reflected this constant. Such stability, with other factors taken into account (such as local demographics of the population and economic stability), enabled us to estimate probable employee usage of a service.

Certain demographic information can be critical. For example, whether parents are married with two incomes, or the single sole support of their families helps determine the type of care needed and what employees can pay for care. The author's experience is that single parents (who are mostly women) tend to have family incomes that are one-third of those of married parents. Sick child care may be an especially difficult problem for these parents because they may have to pay an additional fee for the care. Transporting children to and from care may also be an added burden for these parents who may not have another adult to share the responsibilities.

Data should also be organized by job category. You can find out what problems are common among certain workers. For example, clerical staff may find that cost of care is a serious problem while professional staff may be more concerned with convenience.

Satisfaction with child care arrangements is an important consideration. Generally, most parents report that they are satisfied with their care, overall. It is believed that many parents will stay with a "known quantity" even though it is not ideal and may in fact present many difficulties, rather than admit their doubts or dissatisfaction. However, when specific aspects of the care are identified, parents can report their areas of dissatisfaction. For example, one parent said that while her caregiver was reliable and punctual, she did not know what the caregiver did with the child during the day and was concerned about the quality of care. Aspects of care that parents may or may not be satisfied with are quality, affordability, convenience, reliability, and hours.

How care was found is another question that can yield useful information. In one study that the author conducted, the vast majority of employees found care informally, through relatives and neighbors. These parents tended to distrust professional or outside resource and referral agencies because of child abuse scandals they had heard about. Again, special efforts must be made to communicate to employees the advantages of specific services.

The questionnaire can elicit estimates from employees about how much work time they spend on child care concerns, how many days they are absent because of child care problems, and whether they have considered quitting their jobs because of child care concerns.

However, to answer these questions honestly, employees must feel that their answers are completely confidential, and that they won't be penalized for telling the truth. With this data, it is possible to figure out (1) the approximate dollar loss per hour or day caused by employee absenteeism due to child care problems, (2) the additional cost of hiring temporary help (when this is done), and (3) if employees leave because of such problems, the loss to the company in terms of recruitment and training of new employees.

Information can be solicited about the influence of a child care service on employees' decisions to return to work after giving birth or adopting a child. Questions about whether employees would return to work sooner if quality child care were available can further help you plan a program.

A group to pay attention to is those who are now pregnant or adopting children within the next several months. These employees are the most likely to take advantage of an infant care service, if one is to be provided within the year.

Another group to identify is parents who have children with special needs. In many communities, parents have great difficulty finding care for children who have physical, emotional, or intellectual disabilities, adding to an already stressful situation. Sometimes, programs are available but parents are unaware of them. The company can provide the information to parents who need it.

Format. The format for the questionnaire is determined by the educational level of the employees to be surveyed, and the degree to which they are familiar with survey tools. Professionals will be more likely to fill out extensive, complex questionnaires. Overall, the survey should not take more than 20 minutes to fill out. If longer, the number of responses drops.[6]

The wording of specific questions depends on whether or not you are using a computer to analyze the results. If you are you should work closely with your consultant and a computer analyst for two reasons. First, answers to the questions must be coded so that the data you want can be easily retrieved from computer tapes. Second, you will want to be sure the questions are worded so that answers will be brief and entirely unambiguous. (A separate place can be left at the end of the questionnaire for longer comments.)

It is a good idea to sample test the questionnaire. Include employees from the various job categories. Find out how much time was needed, whether questions were clearly written and easy to understand and answer, and whether employees felt comfortable about answering them.

Questions to Ask.   The content of your questionnaire should be determined by the options that are under consideration. Management's input will have helped you define the limits. For example, if management has decided that under no circumstances can the company support the creation of an on-site child care center, you would not ask, "Would you be interested in enrolling your child in an on-site child care center?"

Use common sense in designing questions. Do not ask, for example, "What do you think you should pay for child care?" Most people will answer, "Nothing."

Be sure the meanings of the words you use are clear. "Day care" once meant "publicly funded all-day child care." Today, many people refer to any child care program whether public or private as "day care." To be on the safe side, use "child care" throughout.

A careful choice of questions can yield a great deal of interesting, useful information. For example, if you ask respondents how long they have been with the company, you can compare the needs of long-term employees with those of the recently hired.

In preparing the questionnaire, include questions about issues that arose during interviews with employees. For example, if your employees were concerned about care for sick children, be sure to ask what they do when their child or the caregiver is sick, and what alternatives they would consider under these circumstances. Generally, the questionnaire should cover the following topics:

1. Demographics—gender, age, home address and zip code, means of getting to work, marital status, total family income, number and ages of children, type of care used, hours, cost, and how care was found.

2. Attitudes—preference for care regarding type, location, and cost. Ask specific questions about what "quality care" means to them. Try to determine if people would be willing to participate in setting up and operating a program.

3. Connection between child care needs and work problems—when working mothers returned from maternity leave, how long it took to find care, absenteeism or lateness owing to child care problems, morale, and attitudes toward a company that provides support for working parents.

4. Special issues—children with special needs, sick child care, personal leave for child care, desire for flexible hours, part-time or at-home work, and interest in educational materials about parenting and child care.

Sample Questionnaire Items.   Adapt these to your situation by changing the order, phrasing, and so on. Use multiple choice answers. (Note: include a statement of purpose and instructions for completing and returning the questionnaire.)

1. Do you have children under 15 living with you? (If not, please answer *only* questions 2 through 8.)

2. What is your job category? (Exempt, nonexempt, manager, union, etc.)

3. What is your job title? Department? Location (if more than one site)?

4. What hours do you regularly work? What days?

5. Do you work full- or part-time?

6. How long have you worked for the company?

7. Has your work been more difficult during the last year owing to other employees' child care problems?

8. What is your gender and age?

9. Do you plan to have children within the next five years?

10. Are you married, living with another adult, or single?

11. If you are married, is your spouse employed? Full-time?

12. How much of the time does your child live with you?

13. What is your zip code?

14. How do you get to work?

15. What is your total family income? (Include that of all adults in your household, *before* taxes.)

16. List the birthdays for each child under 15 living with you.
    Child no. 1 _____ no. 2 _____ etc.

17. How is each child currently cared for while you work? (Include after school, summer, etc.)

18. What days do you usually need child care for each child? Hours?

19. What is the average monthly amount you spend for the care of all your children while you work? (Include summer care, sick care, etc.)

20. Is the care for your child(ren) located near work? Near home?

21. How did you find your current child care arrangements? How much time did you spend?

22. What do you like most about each arrangement? Least? (cost, location, quality, etc.)

23. Approximately how many times in the last month were you late to work, had to leave early, etc. because of child care problems?

24. Approximately how many days in the last year were you absent because of child care difficulties?

25. Who usually cares for your children when they are sick?

26. How many times have you changed child care arrangements in the last two years?

27. Indicate preference of care for each child (someone in my home, care in someone else's home, child care center).

28. Given some of the common problems related to child care for working parents (quality, cost, location, dependability, transportation, finding appropriate care for

child of each age, scheduling, sick child care, etc.) which have been most difficult within the last year?

29. If you could get the kind of child care you want at a reasonable cost, how would it affect your job? (change shifts, work full-time, etc.)

30. Would you prefer a child care center near work?

31. Would you attend workshops on child care if they were available during working hours at your work site?

32. Would you like to have written information about parenting and child care?

33. Would you like to have professional help to locate appropriate child care? (resource and referral).

34. If any of your children have special needs, indicate what they are.

35. How satisfied are you with your work hours? If you could, how would you change them?

36. Do you feel "supported" by your supervisor in terms of your child care needs?

37. What are your suggestions or comments?

Who Should Be Given the Questionnaire.   In general, it is a good idea to survey all employees. Some companies with more than 3,000 employees survey a sample, usually 10 percent.[7] Random samples of individual employee groups may be surveyed, for example, exempt and nonexempt. On the other hand, specific employee groups, such as clerical women, can be surveyed more extensively than others, if they are perceived to have greater child care needs.

Sometimes it is wise to survey all employees but to analyze only a random sample of questionnaires. In this way, all employees feel that they are taking part in the project.

Advertising the Questionnaire.   People must be made aware of the questionnaire. They need to feel sure that their answers will be kept confidential but that they will be listened to. In alerting employees about the questionnaire, determine the usual channels for advertising similar events to employees. In many companies, the in-house newsletter is read eagerly by all. In others, interoffice memos or bulletin boards are the vehicles for important announcements. In explaining the questionnaire, face-to-face meetings are especially useful.

All of these methods can be carefully timed to reinforce each other. You can begin with a general announcement in the newsletter, followed by bulletin board announcements and interoffice memos, and finally, explanations in greater detail at face-to-face meetings. You should solicit the help of department heads and office managers in checking that the questionnaires were received and in encouraging employees to fill out and return them. The task force or committee can be instrumental in maintaining high visibility for the questionnaire.

Do not let too much time pass between the initial announcement and the actual dissemination of the questionnaire—at most two or three weeks. Otherwise people will forget about it. Announcements should include the purpose of the questionnaire, when it will be given out, how and when it will be collected, and when people will be informed of the results. If there is a delay in analyzing the results, be sure to tell people that the survey is being analyzed and thank them for their cooperation.

Printing the Questionnaire.   Keep the questionnaire as brief as possible while asking all the necessary questions. If you are using a computer, be sure you have the right program for it. You may want to put the data through the computer again after you have received the initial results. Be sure provisions are made for this possibility.

A cover letter describing the questionnaire can be on company letterhead or on the consultant's letterhead. The latter distances the company from the survey, assuring employees that it is entirely confidential. The former is probably more personal. Explain that the survey is being conducted to find out what child care needs employees have and that the company does not yet know how it will be able to respond.

Dissemination.   While the questionnaire can be made available to employees in areas where they congregate (such as on a table in the company cafeteria), I recommend that you directly present each employee with his or her own copy. Questionnaires can be included with employees' paychecks, or they can be mailed to employees' offices or homes.

Collection.   People can fill out the questionnaire on the job—during work time, a coffee break, or lunch—and return it immediately, or you can have employees send it back by mail. The rule of thumb is that returning the questionnaire should require as little effort as possible. Again, involve department heads in collecting the questionnaire, if possible. The Conference Board study found that employers received a return rate of 35 percent to 95 percent, with the majority getting 50 percent.[8] Because of a heavy communications effort with clients, the author has had a high rate of success in return rates (frequently 75 percent).

Analysis.   Your data should give you a picture of the current child care situation of employees and a projection of what the needs will be over the next few years. You can isolate certain variables, such as job category or where people live, and determine the specifics of respondents' situations. If you are considering a service that costs, say, $80 per week, you can identify those who either pay this currently or who, based on family income, could afford it. In this way, you can determine if such a service is feasible. One study conducted by the author identified employees who were interested in placing their young children in a near-site child care center. Although many reported that they would be willing to pay the going rate in the community, their family incomes indicated that the cost would be prohibitive. In designing a program, such information must be taken into account.

The demographic data can help you design options you may not have thought of. For example, suppose a substantial number of employees who live near each other have similar problems with after-school care. If your study of the community revealed an after-school program near where these employees live, you might consider providing some form of transportation to get the children from school to the program.

One study conducted by the author found that many employees in dual-career families with one child felt stressed and worried about the quality of their child care. It became apparent that educational material, workshops, and counseling could go a long way toward relieving their stress as well as helping employees who were planning to have children.

The responses to questions about attitudes can also help you design a program. For example, if parents deem the most important aspect of care to be the "quality," and parents feel that their current arrangements are not high quality, you may consider hiring an expert child care trainer to upgrade the quality of nearby centers or family day care programs.

If parents express a preference for child care near home and most of them live a good distance from work, it would make little sense to consider setting up a center at or near work.

If parents indicate a willingness to create or operate a service, you may move in the direction of a parent-owned or parent-run program. Whatever you decide to do, keep your estimates conservative. For example, if 100 people indicate interest in an infant program, plan for 10 or 20 initially. The program can be expanded later as its reputation is established.

Community Resources

Your study should include a careful look at the services that parents are currently using or could use. You should consider even those that at first glance seem inappropriate. You may be able to adapt them. If you decide to visit programs, go with your consultant. For a detailed discussion of what to look at in a child care program, see Chapter 6.

Which Communities Should Be Surveyed?

Most employers begin by looking at the community in which the company is located, followed by neighborhoods where clusters of parents reside. You will need to know what child care networks serve these areas. You may be able to build on programs that are well organized, even if they are located outside the target neighborhood.

How Can Existing Programs Be Adapted to the Needs of Employees?

To adapt an existing program to your employees' needs, find out if it would want to expand. Is space available for expansion? Does it need renovation? If the curriculum is not suitable or the teachers are not trained adequately (for example, to care for infants), what would upgrading cost? If the hours of the program do not coincide with the hours of your employees, what would it cost to change the former? Will the program require financial assistance to meet your employees' needs or will in-kind services be sufficient? If a program has vacancies or is willing to expand, you may be in a good bargaining position. In exchange for providing a product or service such as nursing consultants, special materials, and so on, the company may be able to get special consideration for employees who use or could use the program. If you are considering a child care center or expansion of one that is already in the community, look for space that can house children—in underutilized schools or shopping centers, for example. Worksheet 19 will help you organize the data and analyze it in terms of costs and benefits.

Recommendations

Recommendations to the company should be based on a synthesis of information about the company's perspective, parents' needs, and community services.

You can pare down the range of options to those the company is prepared, philosophically and financially, to consider. The results of the questionnaire should identify the most pressing needs of the population you are most interested in. You can add to the recommendations any information about existing programs that you consider appropriate—for example, providers who have a reputation for "quality" and who are willing to adapt to the needs of your parents, or your consultant can design a new program that meets your objectives, including services that help parents become educated consumers of child care and more effective workers and parents.

One consideration is whether or not community families will be included in the service. If so, you should obtain data about these needs so that the service is designed with them in mind as well. One hospital developed a child care center when it became clear that there was a need not only among its own employees but within the wider community. While hospital employees get priority, they also pay 20 percent less for the service than community families do. The community is affluent and the higher costs are in line with community prices for child care.

It is also important to identify child care efforts already initiated in the community. For example, a group of downtown employers in a large eastern city became interested in the issue for their employees at the same time that the mayor was planning a breakfast for CEOs on the topic. The groups were able to collaborate and work together toward a plan of action.

It is also important to realistically evaluate these efforts. A study by the author found a local resource and referral agency involved in several exciting initiatives to expand child care in the community. On closer examination, however, it became clear that nearly the entire staff of the agency had quit during the last year to move into higher paying public school teaching jobs. Needless to say, progress on the child care initiatives had been severely slowed down.

Among a specific employee population, there can be great differences in availability of services for specific age groups based on where employees live. In one community within the Washington, D.C. area, part-day nursery school is the norm. Parents struggle with "packages" of arrangements for their children, while in other nearby jurisdictions, all-day care, including care for school-age children, is available.

One client of the author's had some employees living in an intensely urban environment, with a range of costly child care options, while others lived in rural communities with almost no child care. Care that was available was, however, quite inexpensive. Both groups' needs had to be addressed.

A good way to begin a new venture is with a pilot project. A pilot would be limited in size and carefully monitored at each stage. Although initially only a limited number of employees will be served, a well-designed pilot program can be expanded to serve a larger population.

DESIGNING AND IMPLEMENTING THE PROGRAM

The Design

Once your recommendations have been approved, you will need to design a program; Worksheet 20 provides an outline. Whether you solicit proposals from outside agents or prepare your own, the written plan should include the following:

Description of the Need

The need should be described, combining data from your needs assessment and your survey of community services. Be as explicit as possible. Use statistics and anecdotal examples to define groups needing services and to show how this need relates to the company's goals and objectives. For example, you may state that parents of infants and toddlers are in serious need of service because few licensed caregivers exist in the community (give the exact number). You may have found that many of these parents are professional women, who have been with the company for a number of years (give figures). If the company is seeking to retain these women, management will want to know that a child care program for infants and toddlers at the work site is preferred by a majority of them (give exact percentage).

Goals and Objectives

You need to clearly state your company's motivating goals, for example, to respond to the needs of dual-career couples, to reduce the turnover of clerical staff, and so on. You also need to state the objectives of the recommended program; for example, to provide parents of infants and toddlers with child care at or near the work site, or to provide all parents with information about what quality child care is.

It is possible to compare the costs and benefits of each child care option under consideration. A cost/benefit analysis can be designed to quantify how such things as absenteeism and turnover rate may be affected.[9]

Method

For the method, you should describe the specific plan to achieve your goals and objectives. Try to build in flexibility, and start small. To reduce turnover, you might, for example, describe hiring a firm to create a child care information service (R&R) that would identify family day care homes near the work site and provide them with start-up funds and training in exchange for giving preference to your employees. Include who will provide the service; how they will do it; how many parents will be served; what relationship the service will have to the company; when the service will be initiated and the timetable for later phases; and how quality will be ensured and the company protected from liability.

Include plans for publicizing the service to potential users, whether current or prospective employees, community residents, and so forth. Decide how employees will be selected for the service—first come first served, a percentage of each employee group, or other criteria. A clear statement of the enrollment policies of the program must be made to potential users to avoid disappointment and frustration if more employees are interested than can be served.

Budget

The budget should include estimated costs, possibly in the form of a range.

Costs. If appropriate, as in the creation of a new child care center or a family day care network, costs can be divided into start-up and operating expenses. (Start-up may include renovation costs, equipment costs, and consultant fees. Operating expenses may include personnel costs, the costs of materials, rent, utilities, and administration, and legal, accounting, and insurance fees.) In other cases, such as a series of workshops, the costs may be stated as one figure.

Payments. Expenses should be broken down to show the part the company will pay, the part parents will pay (if any), and any other sources of funding, such as government or foundation. Further, you may suggest ways of lowering costs to the company, such as providing a revolving loan or in-kind services to the recommended program. Be sure to include information on tax advantages to the company, as well as a discussion of legal issues and how they can be handled.

Evaluation

A plan for evaluation should be an integral part of your recommendation. The plan should be designed with your goals and objectives in mind. The tools used for evaluation may include checklists, written or oral reports, observations, interviews, comparison of data before and after the service was initiated, and so on.

Your consultant can help you select the most appropriate combination of techniques to evaluate your program. In general, the evaluation should include two parts. Part 1 should address the question of whether the service is actually doing what it is supposed to do, that is, meeting your objectives (the expressed needs of the targeted group). Part 2 should look at the effectiveness of the program in meeting the broader goals of the company.

Part 1.   To determine if your program is proceeding as planned, you will have to match performance with objectives, as defined in the Method section. Did the firm or individual hired perform the tasks that you contracted for in the time frame you expected? If not, why not? You will also want to know whether the service is actually meeting the needs of the targeted group. How many parents have used the service? What was their reaction to it? How might the program be made more responsive to the needs of employees?

In this part, you should show how you are going to obtain the data. You can have the provider record his or her activities and give the record to you periodically. You should solicit parents' reactions, either through interviews or in written form, by having them fill out checklists or comment sheets.

Assessment by parents is essential. Some may prefer to remain anonymous for fear that negative comments will be made known to the provider. Decide how frequently you want to solicit parent reactions. During the early months, you may want to do this more often, say, every three months. Since most programs take several months to gel, the feedback should be designed to be constructive, not merely negative. You may ask for "suggestions" rather than "complaints." For example, questions might include: How did you hear about the program? What made you choose it? What do you like most about it? What suggestions, if any, do you have to make it work better for you?

Part 2.   Start with a restatement of what the company hopes to achieve, and set up a "before" and "after" comparison. If you are looking for improvement in recruitment, turnover rate, or absenteeism, you need prior documentation for comparison. If the statistics show a change for the better, you will want to interview or poll employees to confirm that the program is responsible for the changes. For example, when new people are hired, they should be asked whether they knew about the service and, if they did know, how it influenced their choice to take the position. Similarly, if your primary concern is workforce morale, you can poll a random sample of employees throughout the company and compare their responses with those of employees before the program was instituted.

You can also compare certain variables, such as absenteeism and tardiness among parents using the service, parents not using the service, and the rest of the employee population. While these may be rough comparisons, because you may not be able to control for ages of children and so on, they will give you a "feel" for the program's effectiveness.

If the company's goals concern the larger community (for example, a more favorable image among local taxpayers), you might interview by telephone a random sample of community residents, merchants, and so on, both before and after the inception of the service, asking if their attitude toward the company has changed as a result of the program.

Implementation

A company liaison needs to coordinate the new service with the employees using it and the company. An advisory committee, made up of the original task force and parents using the service, can oversee the project with the cooperation of the company liaison. The committee can review reports, and make suggestions to the provider and recommendations to the company. You will want to communicate regularly with the provider of the service. Sometimes a minor adjustment can have a tremendous impact on the success of a program. For example, if only parents of infants and toddlers are attending workshops, it may be that parents of school-age and adolescent children are simply not aware that the workshops are also designed for them. In this case, you would need to send out a clarifying memo.

A new service frequently is slow to gather momentum. Thus, even though parents could benefit from the family day care network you have developed, they may be reluctant to get involved since the concept is unfamiliar to them. Again, you may need to publicize more heavily, distribute a pamphlet about the service, show pictures, and so on. Eventually, word of mouth will disseminate the news, but this may take longer than you think.

You will have to continue to market the service, especially if it is off-site, since new parents may not be aware of it. Articles about the program should be placed in the in-house newsletter periodically; fund-raisers and other program events can provide an opportunity to remind all employees about the service. Worksheet 21 can be used to document the program's implementation and progress.

A final report would include a summary of what actually happened and an evaluation of how well the program achieved both its objectives and the company's goals. It may be that the plan was a good one, but that the particular individual providing the service was not able to do the job. In this case, do not scrap the plan. Look for other individuals to implement it. Include recommendations and modifications (see Worksheet 22).

Worksheet 16
Record of Task Force Activities

Document the activities of the task force on child care.

Overall goals:

Specific objectives:

1.

2.

3.

Task: e.g. Identify resource and referral programs

Member responsible:

Phone no:

Date due:

Findings:

Next step:

Worksheet 17
Selecting a Consultant

Name:

Organization:

Referred by:

Specific Areas of Expertise (e.g., quality child care, fringe benefits, communications, legal/insurance, consortia, etc.):

Credential:

Clients:

Publications:

Fees:

Comments:

Worksheet 18
Informal Needs Assessment

Information from workshops and/or targeted groups can help you identify
child care concerns.

Report of targeted groups and/or workshops

Topic: Date:

Number of participants:

Main points:

1.

2.

3.

Concerns expressed:

1.

2.

Follow-up notes:

Worksheet 19
Investigating the Range of Options

Compare the cost/vs. savings of each option:

	Costs				Savings in			
Start Up	Commun- ications	Ongoing Costs	Per Emplvee	Absen- teeism	Turn. over	Rec uit	"P. R"	Product tivity

Flex Time/
Job Sharing, etc.

Parttime
Work

Maternity/
Paternity
Leave
-with pay
-without pay

Adoption
Reimb.

Child care
Reimb.

Workshops/
Seminars

R&R

Family Day
Care Network

Center
-infant,toddler,
- preschool
-school-age

Sick Care

Transportation

Other

Following is an outline for organizing the information you need to design your program:

I. The Need

Demographics of employees
Summary of community child care programs
Relationship to company goals

II. Goals and Objectives

Long-range company goals
Immediate objectives of a service

III. Method

Type of service
Provider of the service
Plan for the service
Relationship to the company
Time frame (when and for how long)
How initiate

IV. Budget

Itemized cost of the service
Consulting fees
Funding options
Tax options/advantages

V. Evaluation

Usage
Achievement of goals and objectives
Cost/benefit analysis

VI. Implementation

This form will help you document how the program you implement is progressing and how well it is achieving your company's goals.

Date:

Description of what has happened (objectives achieved; changes made, etc.)

No. of parents served:

Reactions of parents (how obtained):

Impact on productivity (absenteeism, recruitment, turnover, etc.)"

Recommendations:

Worksheet 22
Final Report

Following is an outline for a final report. Individual progress reports can be attached for further documentation.

I. Summary of the program (Attach progress reports)

Background
Goals
Who provided
When
How
Cost
Who used it

II. Evaluation (Attach documentation - questionnaires, interview forms, etc.)

How closely did the program follow the plan?
What problems arose and how were they solved/not solved?
What was found to be most effective in terms of objectives achieved, goals reached?
Parents' reactions; company reactions; community reactions
Needs that surfaced

III. Recommendations

Next year
Next 5 years, etc.

Date_____   Submitted by_____

NOTES

1. Jacquelyn McCroskey, "Work and Families: What Is the Employer's Responsibility?" *Personnel Journal*, January 1982, p. 33.

2. Friedman, *Family-Supportive Policies*, p. 12.

3. Ibid., p. 13.

4. Ibid., p. 13.

5. Herbert Bienstock, "Rationale for Corporate Involvement," speech given at the New York City Chamber of Commerce on Employer-Supported Child Care, November 22, 1981.

6. Friedman, *Family-Supportive Policies*, p. 23.

7. Ibid., p. 22.

8. Ibid., p. 25.

9. Burud, Aschbacher, and McCroskey, *Employer-Supported Child Care*, p. 49.

6

QUALITY CHILD CARE

Throughout this book we have referred to "quality care." It is now time to explain what quality child care is, why it is so important, and how it can be secured.

THE IMPORTANCE OF QUALITY CARE

Quality child care makes the difference between parents whose minds are not on the job because they are worried about their children, and parents who feel at ease about their children and are able to devote full attention to their work. An understanding of quality child care can help a company determine which of several options to provide for parents. In a study of employer-supported child care centers that failed, it was found that a major reason for failure was that parents perceived the center as low in quality.[1]

An employer would also want to be associated only with high quality child care programs since these are more likely to meet the standards of insurers in today's tight insurance market. Such standards assure that the program will be a safe and healthy one for children, parents, and staff, and that the employer supporting the program will have reduced risk and minimal problems with liability.

Quality child care is care that is not merely babysitting or custodial. Such programs are of negative value for children. Rather, it is care that recognizes the basic developmental needs of children and provides a stimulating and supportive environment that meets these needs.

A concerned company can improve the quality of an existing program. It can provide grants to raise the quality of care. Caregivers can be trained to provide developmental care for children and emotional support for their parents. In general, the program can be enriched so that it is more stimulating to children.

Information about quality child care can be provided in written form and through consultation with experts. The information can focus on what to look for in programs and care providers.

Any individual, committee, or task force that is exploring the options for corporate support of working parents must have some idea what quality child care is. Considerations of "quality" must help shape the decision making, along with considerations of employees' specific child care needs, the kinds of services available, and the costs of care.

It is becoming more and more important to recognize quality care when you see it, since federal guidelines concerning quality are no longer reliable. The federal government in the past set standards for the many programs it funded. With a 20 percent cut in the social service budget and funds no longer going directly to individual programs (the states receive block grants instead), the federal government is practically out of the business of regulating and monitoring care. Private organizations such as the National Association for the Education of Young Children (NAEYC) have developed accreditation systems for providers but these are not yet as widely accepted as they need to be.

Here are some guidelines for looking at child care programs. Worksheets 23, 24, and 25 are provided to fill out while observing a program or caregiver. This can be helpful when presenting information to a committee or group.

Parents' Point of View

Aside from the practical aspects of a program, such as the cost, hours, proximity to work or home, ages of the children served, and how these factors match parents' needs, attention must also be given to what parents say they want. Some prefer a "structured" approach, in which the child's day is composed of discrete time periods for specific activities. Others prefer a more fluid approach, with emphasis on activities that the child initiates. Most educators would agree that while good programs can be built around either approach, neither extreme—excessive regimentation or total lack of direction—is compatible with quality.

If a company wants to ensure that working parents will use a company-supported child care service, the opinions of the parents must be taken into account before arrangements are completed. This is especially true of new programs. Parents are understandably reluctant to buy into a program that they have not seen. Similarly, if the company is considering providing funds, buying slots, or giving other support to an existing program, it should solicit the opinions of parents who are already using the service.

THE DIFFERENT KINDS OF CHILD CARE PROGRAMS

Child care programs vary according to the ages of the children served, hours of operation, purpose and philosophy, and funding. Today, most try to provide an educational program, since much research shows that very young children are capable of an enormous amount of learning. A good educational program is one that respects the developmental level of a child; that is, the providers recognize that young children learn not by passively absorbing information, but by active exploration within a supportive environment.

Researchers, such as Jerome Kagan of Harvard, have shown that high quality group care has as an equally beneficial effect on children's development as being at home with the parent.[2] More recently, other researchers have found that children in higher quality centers fair better socially, intellectually, and in their communication skills than children in lower quality centers.[3]

SERVICES FOR DIFFERENT AGE GROUPS

Services may be for profit or not for profit; they may be funded entirely by parent fees, by the federal and/or state government, or by a private foundation, such as the Catholic Charities, the United Way, or the Federation of Jewish Philanthropies. Although "quality" is not determined by the type or source of funding, the philosophy of a program may be influenced by this. For example, a program that is supported by a church may have a religious component. You should familiarize yourself with the differences between various programs— their goals, curriculum design, parent participation requirements, fees, and so on.

Programs differ as to the ages of children served, the hours of operation, and the provision of meals and other support services. For example, some programs provide social and medical services for families, while others provide financial subsidies or scholarships for families that qualify. Private nursery schools differ from day care centers in that they offer morning or afternoon sessions, although some day care centers offer part-time care.

PREFERENCE FOR CARE

Infants and Toddlers

In general, working parents of infants and toddlers have the fewest child care options. Most infants and toddlers of working parents are cared for informally in family day care homes or by relatives, sometimes in parents' own homes. Only a small number are in child care centers or in licensed care of any kind. Few publicly funded programs for working parents accommodate infants. Data analyzed by Sandra Hofferth and Deborah Phillips show that center care for infants is growing at a faster rate than family day care or in-home care.[4]

Preschoolers (three- to five-year-olds)

Preschoolers may be cared for in family day care homes, day care centers, federally funded Head Start programs, private nursery schools, or some public school systems. Sometimes a preschool center also accommodates infants and toddlers. Increasingly, more highly educated, higher-income parents are choosing center care for their preschoolers.[5]

School-Age Children

To conform to parents' work schedules, before-school programs for children who attend regular elementary school (ages 6 to 12) start as early as 7:00 A.M. After-school programs may end as late as 6:30 P.M. If these programs are in local public schools, they may also be run by a nonprofit agency such as the Young Men's Christian Association or a for-profit company that offers instruction in a sport, craft, or drama. Family day care homes frequently offer care for school-age children. The same kinds of programs offer care during holidays and the summer, as do preschool child care centers and nurseries.

Special summer programs include camps, programs in public schools or parks, and private elementary schools.

Children With Special Needs

Programs for children who have hearing, visual, motor, or other developmental difficulties may be found in private, nonprofit, or for-profit schools, hospitals, or public schools. Parents may qualify for special funds to cover care for their children with special needs.

In some communities such care is hard to come by, particularly if children have chronic illnesses that require special medication or treatment. Sometimes children with special needs are "mainstreamed" into regular classrooms. The experience can be an enriching one for all the children. However, adaptations must be made in the environment and additional teachers, specially trained to meet the needs of these children, must be included in the program.

Quality early childhood programs have staff members who are trained to identify children with special needs. Many programs test all children to screen for those who might have developmental lags or problems. Since young children can learn skills to help them cope more effectively with a special problem, early detection programs are an important component of child care.

Sick Children

Parents usually stay home with their very ill children. However, many parents would return to work if they could find care for their children who are no longer contagious and are recovering from an illness or injury. There are about 80 programs across the country that care for sick or "mildly ill" children. Most are in hospitals, frequently in an unused wing. Several consist of caregivers trained to go into the home to care for the children (see Chapter 4).

Few guidelines have been developed for such care. Some conditions to consider are:

1. The child should be familiar with the program or caregiver and should have visited several times when not ill. Sick children are more irritable and may have an especially difficult time in an entirely new environment or with a "stranger" staying with them in their home.

2. Parents should describe symptoms over the phone to avoid unnecessarily moving a sick child if the program is inappropriate. Children should be screened by a doctor or nurse before being admitted to a program. During pre-enrollment in a program, parents should receive guidelines for admittance to the program.

3. The program or caregiver should provide a program of rest and quiet play. Toys and other items used by children in sick care programs should be sterilized after use.

4. Caregivers must be trained to support children and understand that their emotional needs may be greater at this time than when they are well.

5. Parents should be kept informed of children's condition throughout the day. They should be notified if there is a change in condition.

COST OF CHILD CARE

Child care programs vary considerably in what they charge parents. Most charge a fixed fee that is usually based on the child's age: care for younger children, who require a higher ratio of adults, costs more than care for older children. Programs that are heavily funded by a charitable agency or by the government may also be able to keep fees down. A few programs charge on a sliding scale based on family income. In addition to the basic fee, there may be extra charges for before- and after-program hours (say 7:00 to 9:00 A.M. or 3:00 to 6:00 P.M.), transportation, and trips. Most programs charge parents when their children are out sick or on vacation, to cover their fixed expenses. (For parents of a sick child, this may be a double expense, because they may have to pay a babysitter as well.) Some programs expect parents to make an additional donation in the form of a tax-deductible gift. Some charge a late fee if parents come to pick up their children after closing hours. This may seem harsh, but the teachers themselves may be working parents who have to get home and care for their own children.

The cost of care varies across the country, ranging roughly from $40 to $200 per week per child, with family day care usually the least expensive and infant care the most expensive. A caregiver in a person's own home may cost as much as $350 per week, but this often includes homemaking services as well as care for other children in the family.

One way of lowering the cost of care is by developing a parent cooperative. Unlike earlier models, in which parents rotated helping out in the classroom, the "'80s" coop has parents participating by taking on routine tasks that they can perform during nonwork hours, such as doing laundry, shopping for food, building maintenance, and fixing equipment. (Such a model is the Senate Child Care Center: see Chapter 4.) These activities also result in greater parent involvement.

ADMINISTRATIVE POLICIES OF THE PROGRAM

Child care providers have a wide variety of rules regarding the admission and expulsion of children, parent involvement, holiday closings, and so on. Programs may expel children if parents have not paid the fees for a certain number of days or weeks, or if a child is disruptive. It is important to know what a program is prepared to do to help a family meet its financial commitment or to cope with a child who is having behavioral problems. Many providers refer families to appropriate counseling or psychological services within the community.

INSURANCE

In recent years, providers of child care, like providers of health care, have had difficulty obtaining liability insurance. Premium costs for child care programs have skyrocketed, presumably based on claims paid by insurers. However, it is not clear what research has been used to justify these costs. Any employer who plans to be involved with a child care program needs to be sure that the program has adequate coverage. This should include property and casualty, vehicle, accidental death and dismemberment, and other relevant coverage. Insurers such as Markedyne and Nautilus have created packages for child care centers which can be obtained through the National Association for the Education of Young Children or through the company itself.

HOW CHILDREN LEARN

There are several different philosophies of child care: Montessori, traditional, Piagetian, open, and others. Basic to all, however, is a respect for the child and the child's needs. Children need to use materials actively, to exercise their bodies, and to initiate their own learning experiences.

Young children need to be with adults who explain things to them, who ask questions, who listen to their ideas, and who encourage them to relate to one another warmly and honestly. While young children do not actually "share" possessions, they can learn to take turns and to respect the needs of other children.

HEALTH AND SAFETY POLICIES

Child care providers should adhere to strict rules and procedures for maintaining a clean, safe environment. Staff must pass regular medical examinations and be immunized against certain illnesses, just as do the children in their care. Hand washing by staff and children, particularly when dealing with diapering and food handling, is the most important way to prevent the spread of infection.[6]

A policy for sick children should be articulated, whether children are placed in a special area away from the other children, removed to another center, or taken home by a parent or guardian. Sick children should be isolated from the rest of the group but not be left unsupervised.

Research shows that many accidents and injuries can be avoided if the indoor and outdoor space, and equipment and materials are designed to follow strict guidelines for type of materials used, size, height, condition, placement, and so on. Children must be carefully supervised indoors and out, and be taught to follow rules of safety while using equipment.

TRANSPORTATION

Find out how children get to and from the program. Is it near public transportation? Can parents use car pools? Does the program offer a bus service? If not, can it recommend one?

REPUTATION: PARENT SATISFACTION

Different programs have different "personalities" based on their goals and the nature of the communities they serve. It is helpful to know how long a program has been in operation, and how long the present director, board, or owner has been in charge.

How Do Parents in a Given Community Find Out about Child Care?

Each community has its own system of providing information about programs to parents. In rare cases, such as Central Florida's 4Cs (Community Coordinated Child Care), computerized services not only list programs but also perform centralized billing and vacancy control. In the twin cities of Minneapolis and St. Paul, corporations donate to a central listing organization, Resources for Parents, which is run by a community agency. In New York City, both the ACD and Child Care, Inc., provide information and referral services. In general, it is not easy to obtain information about child care programs. You will probably have to do some digging. Women's associations, chambers of commerce, the NAEYC, the Day Care Council, the United Way, the Health Department, and local licensing agencies are all organizations that can help you locate child care.

Regulations for programs vary throughout the country. Many centers are licensed, but family day care homes may simply be registered. Check Appendix A to find the agency within your state that handles regulations.

MEANING OF A LICENSE

A program with a license has met some minimum standards usually established by a state agency. The standards concern physical space and equipment, teacher-to-child ratio, health requirements, teacher credentials, food, children's activities, administrative procedures, record keeping, and so forth. However, licensing is but one determinant of the quality of a program. Since standards vary from state to state and, in some instances, from locale to locale, the best way to evaluate a program is to see it for yourself.

FIELD VISITS

In a field visit, start by talking with someone in a position of responsibility. Do not hesitate to ask a lot of questions (Worksheet 23 provides a list). Find out about the goals for children and how these are reflected in the program. Do the answers make sense to you? Do they coincide with views that parent-employees have expressed? Ask for a copy of any written material the center or program may have. Policy guides and written material about curriculum can be especially informative.

Find out what kind of credentials the staff has. Is there ongoing staff training? If so, who conducts the training? Is the center or program affiliated with a college or university that provides support services?

Ask how parents and children are introduced to the program. Are provisions made for parents to stay or visit with their children, especially during the first few days or weeks?

Can parents visit at any time? With recent alarming reports of child abuse in so-called reputable centers, an open visiting policy for parents is a must.

When you are looking at family day care, find out who else (besides the primary provider) is on call if a child is injured or if the caregiver is sick. What is the policy regarding sick children?

Take time—an hour should be sufficient—to observe the program in action. Try to sit in each room for about 15 minutes so that you can get a feeling for the physical setting, the caregivers, and the curriculum. Use Worksheet 24 as a checklist while observing a program.

The Physical Setting

The way a room is organized determines what children do. Ideally, there should be large areas where children can move about freely and safely, and smaller areas for quiet play. There should be a variety of textures and colors that are stimulating without being overwhelming. Early childhood rooms are usually divided into areas for different kinds of learning; for example, an area with blocks, one for dramatic play (with dress-up clothes, costumes, and props), one for art, music, story, science, and so on. Look at the materials that are offered. Children need "fluid" materials (sand, water, clay, or finger paints) that lend themselves easily to creative expression. (If you see "art" works that all look alike and are based on a teacher's pattern, watch out! This means children are not creating for themselves.)

Children also need "structured" materials (puzzles, blocks, games) so they can learn about organizing and sorting things and ideas. With materials that lend themselves to pretend play (dolls, dress-up clothes, and furniture scaled to their size), children can explore different roles. Materials should be in good condition, with broken parts mended. Each item should be stored in a specific place, and many should be easily accessible to the children. Although children must learn that materials are to be handled carefully, they should also feel free to use those that appeal to them.

The number of children in a room also determines what children can do. In fact, organization in small groups has been found to be one of the important components of high-quality care.[7] If there are too many children, they will find it difficult to use materials or relate to each other effectively. The following groupings (each ideally with 3 adults) can serve as a guide: 15 three-year-olds, 18 four-year-olds, or 25 five-year-olds.

The organization of the room and the materials in it are important because these set the stage for learning. However, it is the people involved—the caregivers—who make the difference between a custodial program and an exciting learning experience. To assess the all-important human factors, you should focus on

1. The way caregivers relate to the children physically;
2. How they talk to the children;
3. What they talk about with the children;
4. The consistency of care; and
5. The caregivers' support of the parents.

One important finding of recent research is that caregivers who are well educated and have had specialized training in early childhood education are associated with high quality child care.[8]

The Caregivers

Relating to Children Physically

Focus on one caregiver at a time. Note whether he or she is close to children—touching them gently—or aloof from them. The younger the children, the more physical contact they need. Many children need to snuggle into a warm lap at some point during the long day, perhaps when a story is being read. Think about whether or not the caregiver seems happy to be there, enjoying the children. Children need to feel cared about.

The Content of the Caregiver-Child Dialogue

Young children learn by talking about what they are doing at the moment. The caregiver should help the child do this. For example, as the child plays with clay, the caregiver might say, "I see you are squeezing the clay. How does it feel? or "You seem to be making something. Can you tell me about it?"

Consistency of Care

In order for children to learn, they must feel good about themselves and the world—they must trust that their needs will be met. For this to happen, children must develop attachments to specific caregivers. Find out how long caregivers have been working in a particular program and how long they intend to stay. Look for programs in which the staff has remained for several years. Where caregivers are paid a minimum wage and given no benefits, staff turnover will be particularly high. Beware of such programs.

Support of Parents

Try to arrange a visit so you can observe caregivers interacting with parents, either when they drop off their children or pick them up. Caregivers should see their role as helping, not competing with, parents. They should be able to share with parents the pleasures of the children's growth. They can do this by giving information—anecdotes of what happened during the day, how the child responded to a new game, what he or she liked or did not like, something new attempted; supporting parents' efforts; discussing ways of handling situations; asking about the routine at home; responding to parents' suggestions in a positive way; and asking how parents feel about what is happening, what they see, and what they want to happen.

The Curriculum

A quality program provides a variety of activities and a balance between active and passive, child- and adult-initiated experiences. Although there should be order to the day, there should also be flexibility so that each child's pace and style of learning are respected. A good program usually hums with activity without being too noisy or too quiet. Most programs have a written schedule prominently posted. Look at it.

If you watch a single child for several minutes, you will get a sense of how the program actually works. Is the child using materials with care or recklessly? If children seem deeply involved in what they are doing, it is a good sign that the program is engaging them. Do they seem relaxed? Do they talk freely with other children and caregivers?

Before you leave, talk again with a representative of the program. Bring up any new questions you may have, such as how the program's goals relate to the specific activities you observed. If you can, talk with the caregivers you observed.

Outdoor Program

Children's outdoor activities in a play area should also be carefully supervised learning experiences. There should be enough space and equipment to stimulate children's imaginations and provide opportunities for learning and practicing new skills.

Climbing equipment should be in good condition, steady and safe. High areas should have railings to prevent falls. Traffic patterns and fences should protect children from equipment, such as swings, that could be harmful. The floor or ground of the play area where children climb should be made of material, such as hard rubber, to cushion falls.

Teachers should be supervising children at all times.

ASSESSING OTHER TYPES OF PROGRAMS: FAMILY DAY CARE, SCHOOL-AGE PROGRAMS, AND INFANT CARE

With some adaptations, the interview (Worksheet 23) and observation (Worksheet 24) forms can be useful in assessing other child care situations. For example, if you are observing someone taking care of a child in the parent's home, look at the way the caregiver arranges the child's space, ask what the caregiver plans to do each day, and observe how these plans are realized. Notice how the caregiver interacts with a child. Does she encourage the child to use materials? Does she talk with the child about what he or she is doing?

For family day care, the same principles apply as for center care, except that the environment should have a more "homelike" feeling. The child still needs space for quiet and for large muscle activities, materials for sensory exploration, books, and so on. The caregiver should take advantage of the range of ages of the children to promote learning—all children benefit when older children help younger children with daily routines. However, older children also need attention and affection, and caregivers should be sensitive to this.

After-school programs should also be examined in terms of the physical environment, caregiver involvement with children, and curriculum. Stimulating activities should be provided. Children should have opportunities to work alone with a material, such as a puzzle or book; to participate in small group activities, such as clay, collage, or sewing; to participate in projects; and to enjoy sports, either individually or as part of a group. Worksheet 25 can help you analyze school-age programs.

Although some children will spend time on homework, most will need a break from school, a relaxed time with friends. Older school-age children can take responsibility for planning and carrying out projects, such as painting a mural or planning a party. Adolescents can provide much needed help to programs with young children or to a community project, such as feeding the homeless. A skilled caregiver for this age group should act as a facilitator and supporter of young people's efforts to gain mastery over materials and activities, and to be involved in meaningful work.

Most programs provide snacks. Check what these are—whether they are nutritious, how they are served, and so forth.

Some after-school programs are organized around special interests, such as sports or drama. Again, look at the quality of the experience for the children. Are they actively involved? Do they receive formal instruction as well as time to practice on their own? Do caregivers attend to them as individuals and help them overcome difficulties?

What Is Infant Care?

Infant care is in great demand. With more and more mothers returning to work soon after giving birth, infants as young as four weeks are spending a great deal of time in the care of people other than their parents. The caregiver may work in the parent's home, in the caregiver's own home, or in a group day care program. Contrary to what many people think, research shows that infants can do as well in group settings as with one caregiver.[9] The determining factor, as always, is the quality of the care they receive. Unfortunately, many people who take care of infants, especially family day care providers and in-home care providers, are neither licensed nor trained. In locales where infant care is lacking, a company may find it a good investment to hire a child care consultant to train caregivers and to develop a network of at-home providers.

While many of the guidelines already discussed apply to infant care, there are additional factors to be aware of when evaluating an infant caregiver or program. Worksheet 26 can be used as a checklist for observing an infant caregiver.

The Physical Setting

The infant center, or the available space in the caregiver's home, should appear homelike. There should be some places that are soft and cozy, perhaps some large pillows and stuffed animals. There should be clean areas for changing diapers. Each infant should have the same crib each day.

For babies starting to crawl or walk, there should be space to move freely and safely, furniture to help stand up with, and areas where toys can be pulled across the floor. Since rocking chairs encourage warm, relaxed relating between caregiver and baby, a rocking chair in the room is a good sign.

The home should be equipped with safety devices such as protective bars on windows and smoke alarms. Electrical appliances, cleaning fluids, and other dangerous items should be out of children's reach. There should be a plan for fast, safe evacuation in case of fire or other emergency.

Group Size and Composition

To maintain a warm, homelike atmosphere, groups should be kept small. State and city agencies that license child care programs limit the number of babies that one adult is allowed to care for. The prescribed ratios vary from locale to locale—typically, from two to five babies (depending on age) per adult. As you observe a particular program, ask yourself whether the adult can realistically provide loving care for the number of babies assigned. While very young infants may sleep a lot (allowing the caregiver time with others), they need stimulation and attention when awake. Older babies who are crawling and exploring need to to be watched carefully. If caregivers seem fatigued, they may be caring for too many babies at once.

Groups may consist of babies of approximately the same age or children of mixed ages (family groupings). Either alternative is acceptable.

Consistency of Care

Infants even more than preschoolers need caregivers whom they can depend on. To encourage the development of close, loving relationships, each baby should have no more than two primary caregivers (depending on the length of shifts). In addition to the regular staff, one or two volunteers who come on a regular basis can enhance the baby's experience, but too many part-time people may confuse and upset a baby.

The Caregiver

Caregivers should enjoy being with babies. They must value each baby's pattern and level of activity—whether sleeping, eating, or crawling, and they must be able to respond to them through a dialogue—a physical and emotional give-and-take, a kind of dance in which each responds to the other's cues. Caregivers should help the infant succeed at a task that he or she sets, whether it is following the caregiver's movement of a bottle with the eyes (in a very young infant) or an older child attempting to feed himself or herself. When with several babies, the caregiver should provide enough toys and materials so that the infants can play side by side without being forced to "share" before they are ready to do so. Caregivers should help infants relate to each other by telling each what the others are doing.

Providing Stimulation

The stimulation that the caregiver provides should match the baby's level of development and encourage him or her to learn about the world through his or her efforts. Too much stimulation can be upsetting and confusing. Too little stimulation will limit the baby's learning. The key is how the caregiver responds to the baby's attempts to communicate and explore. Caregivers should understand and respect the way babies learn. They should be guided by the babies' initiatives, encouraging them by voice and actions. For example, when babies put objects in their mouths, caregivers should accept this behavior as a learning experience. In playing with the baby, the caregiver should provide toys that the infant can manipulate without danger of injury or infection. These should not be too small or sharp. Rather than simply handing the baby the objects, the caregiver should place them within reach so the baby can grasp what he or she wants. The caregiver's mirroring of the baby's motions and phrases should communicate a sense of enjoyment and their special relationship with one another. (See Worksheet 26).

FINAL NOTE

Employer-supported programs for working parents reflect the recognition of the new work force in the United States and the important role that business can and must play in helping parents go to work. In the three years since the first edition of *The Employer's Guide to Child Care*, the author has seen interest in the topic sparked in all fields of work, from high technology to manufacturing, from health care to publishing, from governments to foundations and associations, and from professional partnerships to multinational corporations.

While there is still a long way to go to meet the needs of working parents, business people today no longer seem puzzled when the subject of employer-supported child care is raised. Rather, many have heard about it and want to know more. Many are beginning to apply general knowledge from the field to their own situations.

Besides considering the immediate benefits of employer-supported child care, companies are starting to take a hard look at the role they might play in helping prepare the next generation for life in a complex, demanding world. Our children must be educated to the best of their abilities and with the best that our culture has to offer. Their education begins at birth. Concerned corporations will see to it that children in the United States, the majority of whom have parents in the work force, receive the nurturing, the stimulation, and the solid foundation in learning that they need to maintain this country's place in the future.

Worksheet 23
Interview: Child Care Program Director

When observing a child care program, ask the director or person in charge the following questions. The responses will be helpful in determining the quality of care provided.

Name of Program_____Address/Phone_____

Director_____ Date_____ Submitted by_____

1. Is the program licensed? License No., type, expiration date:

2. Is the program insured? Amount:

3. What are the goals for children?

4. What are the days, hours of operation?

5. What are the scheduled holidays? (Program is closed)

6. What are the tuition fees? Other fees?

7. Is transportation provided? What is the charge?

8. What are the written policies (late arrival, late pick-up, sick child, etc.)?

9. Are parents allowed to visit at any time? Are they required to participate?

10. How is the program funded? Is there any religious affiliation?

11. What activities/materials are provided for children? Indoors/outdoors?

12. What is the staff/child ratio for children of different ages?

13. How long have teachers been here?

14. What are the educational backgrounds (degrees, experience) of teachers? What in-service training (workshops, seminars, etc.) is provided?

15. Describe a typical day for a child in the program.

16. How are discipline problems handled?

17. How are toileting, napping, eating, crying child handled?

Worksheet 24
Observation Form: Preschool Classroom

Name of Program_____Address/Phone_____
Classroom_____Adults_____
Ages of Children_____No. of Children_____Date_____

Check if the room has the following areas:
Active play (floor mat, climbing equip., large space).......... ____yes ____no
Dramatic play (dress up clothes, play furniture, dolls)..... . ____yes ____no
Library, quiet games (books, table games, soft pillows).. ____yes ____no
Art (easels/paint,crayons,clay, collage/paste,finger paint)____yes ____no
Science (water, sand, plants, animals)... ____yes ____no
Music (instruments, sound makers, scarves, record-player) ____yes ____no
Block-building (blocks organized by size,shape,floor space)____yes ____no

The room seems:
very messy____ very neat____ reasonably neat/messy____
very noisy____ very quiet____reasonably quiet/noisy____
safe (no slippery floors, electrical appliances, cleaning supplies away, no
obstructions on floor, etc.)____, unsafe____(list dangers)_____

Children seem:
actively involved in play individually____, in small groups____ both____
not actively involved____(running aimlessly, fighting, etc.)
happy____ unhappy____ can't tell____

Caregivers seem:
involved with children supportively but not intrusively____
not involved with children (talking to each other, doing other work)____
warm, encouraging, playful, friendly____
harsh, cold, angry, unfriendly____
distracted, indifferent____

The room has: enough toys for everyone____ not enough____

The teacher helps children solve problems and arguments by:
talking reasonably with children, listening to both sides____
punishing them without helping them solve the problem____
ignoring them____ other_____

When a child cries, the teacher:
comforts and asks what is wrong____, tells him not to cry or scolds____
ignores the child____

Comments:

Worksheet 25
Information Sheet for School-Age Program

Name of Program_____Address_____
Phone_____   Director_____   Date_____

1. What are the goals of the program?

2. Number and ages of children. How grouped?

3. Days/hours of operation? When closed?

4. What indoor and outdoor space is used?

5. What activites are provided? (e.g. art, cooking, science, music, games, dramatic play, reading, pets, wood working, block building, plays). Is there a balance between quiet and active play? Can children get help with homework?

6. Can children plan their own activities?

7. What snacks are provided and when?

8. Tuition/fees

9. Is transportation provided?

10. How many adults are present?What are their educational backgrounds? Are they involved in staff training?

11. Who sponsors the program? Is there a religious affiliation?

12. What type and amount of insurance does the program have?

13. Is the program licensed? License expires on_____

Comments:

Worksheet 26
Observation of Infant Caregiver

Name of Program_____Address/Phone_____
Classroom_____Adults_____
Ages of Children_____No. of Children_____Date_____

A sensitive, competent caregiver provides a safe, clean environment for babies, warmth and stimulation during play and routines, such as diapering.

The caregiver:

Washes her hands, cleans the changing table after diaper: ___yes ___no

Talks warmly, playfully to baby while diapering, feeding: ___yes ___no

Enables a young baby to watch other children playing (holds in lap, props in infant seat) directs baby's attention to activity: ___yes ___no

Comforts crying baby(holds in arms, soothes, talks gently): ___**yes** ___**no**

Encourages baby to crawl by keeping space clean, free of obstacles; talking to, praising when tries or is successful: ___yes ___no

Teaches simple games, such as "Clap hands," "Bye-bye," sings to baby, repeats baby's coos and sounds: ___yes ___no

Responds to babies as individuals (e.g. sings a "favorite" song to one, puts another to sleep right after feeding, encourages another to crawl, etc.)
                    ___yes ___no

Encourages babies to be independent (e.g. gives finger foods so can feed themselves, toys that they can manipulate themselves):   ___yes ___no

Provides safe, stimulating toys and activities for very young (rattles, mirrors) as well as older babies (books, pull and push toys, dolls, trucks, balls, water toys, stuffed toys, etc.):   ___yes ___no

Has duplicates of "popular" toys so babies don't have to share until ready
                    ___yes ___no

Seems happy to be with babies (talks warmly to them, is alert to their needs, smiles, arranges the environment for their pleasure): ___yes ___no

Comments:

Copyright © 1988 by Barbara Adolf.

NOTES

1. *On-Site Day Care: The State of the Art and Models Development*, Report of the New York State Governor's Office of Employee Relations, Empire State Day Care Services, February 1980, p. 33.

2. Roger Neugebauer, Robert Laurie, Editors, *Caring for Infants and Toddlers: What Works and What Doesn't*, Summit Child Care Center Conference, Summit, New Jersey, April 26–27, 1980, p. 13.

3. Phillips, *Quality in Child Care*, pp. 4–7.

4. Hofferth and Phillips, "Child Care in the United States," p. 562.

5. Andrea I. Burtman, "Who's Minding the Children?" *Working Mother*, April 1984, p. 86.

6. American Academy of Pediatrics, *Health in Day Care: A Manual for Health Professionals*, p. 58.

7. Phillips, *Quality in Child Care*, p. 6.

8. Ibid., p. 7.

9. Burtman, "Who's Minding the Children," p. 86.

APPENDIX A:
CURRENT STATE DAY CARE
LICENSING OFFICES

Department of Human Resources
Division of Family and Children's Services
64 North Union Street
Montgomery, Alabama 36130-1801
(205) 261-5785

Department of Health and Social Services
Pouch H-05
Juneau, Alaska 99811
(907) 465-3206

Arizona Department of Health Services
411 North 24th Street
Phoenix, Arizona 85008
(602) 220-6406

Department of Human Services Pulaski North
1900 Washington Avenue
North Little Rock, Arkansas 72119
(501) 372-2755

Department of Social Services
Community Care Licensing
1315 5th Street, 5th Floor
Sacramento, California 95814
(916) 324-4036

Department of Social Services
Family and Children Services
717 17th Street
Denver, Colorado 80218-0899
(303) 294-5942

State Department of Health Services
Day Care Licensing Unit
150 Washington Street
Hartford, Connecticut 06106
(203) 566-2575

Department of Services for Children, Youth and Families
Licensing Services
330 East 30th Street
Wilmington, Delaware 19802
(302) 571-6436

Department of Consumer and Regulatory Affairs
Service Facility Regulation Administration
Room 1031
Washington, D.C. 20001
(202) 727-7226

Office of Children, Youth and Families
1317 Winewood Boulevard
Tallahassee, Florida 32301
(904) 488-5881

Department of Human Resources
Child Care Licensing Section
878 Peach Tree Street
Room 607
Atlanta, Georgia 30309
(404) 894-5688

Department of Human Services
P.O. Box 339
Honolulu, Hawaii 96809
(808) 548-2302

Department of Health and Welfare
479 Polk Twin Falls
Boise, Idaho 83301
(208) 734-4000

Department of Children and Family Services
406 East Monroe Street
Springfield, Illinois 62701
(217) 785-2688

State Department of Public Welfare
Child Welfare Social Services Division
141 South Meridan Street, 6th Floor
Indianapolis, Indiana 46225
(317) 232-4440

Department of Social Services
3619½ Douglass Avenue
Des Moines, Iowa 50310
(515) 281-5581

Department of Health and Environment
Child Care Licensing Registration
Landon State Office Building
900 Jackson Street
Topeka, Kansas 66620
(913) 296-1270

Department of Human Resources
Division of Licensing and Regulation
275 East Main Street
Frankfort, Kentucky 40621-0001
(502) 564-2800

Department of Health and Human Resources
P.O. Box 3767
Baton Rouge, Louisiana 70821
(504) 342-5774

Department of Human Services
Child Care Licensing Unit
State House Station #11
Augusta, Maine 04333
(207) 289-5060

Department of Health and Mental Hygiene
201 West Preston Street
Baltimore, Maryland 21201
(301) 225-6644

Office for Children
150 Causway Street
Boston, Massachusetts 02114
(617) 727-8900

Michigan Department of Social Services
Child Daycare Licensing Division
300 South Capitol St.
P.O. Box 30037
Lansing, Michigan 48909
(517) 373-8300

Department of Human Services
Division of Licensing & Program Evaluation
444 Lafayette Road
St. Paul, Minnesota 55101
(612) 296-3971

State Board of Health
P.O. Box 1700
Jackson, Mississippi 39205
(601) 960-7740

State Department of Social Services
Broadway State Office Building
P.O. Box 88
Jefferson City, Missouri 65103
(314) 751-2459

Montana Department of Social and Rehabilitation Services
Family Services Department
P.O. Box 8005
Helena, Montana 59604
(406) 444-3865

Department of Social Services
P.O. Box 95026
Lincoln, Nebraska 68509
(402) 471-3121

Division of Youth Services
505 East King Street
Carson City, Nevada 89710
(702) 885-5911

Division of Public Health Services
Bureau of Child Care Standards and Licensing
Hazen Drive
Concord, New Hampshire 03301
(603) 271-4624

Department of Human Services
1 South Montgomery Street
Trenton, New Jersey 08623
(609) 292-1023

Health and Environment Department
1190 St. Francis
P.O. Box 968
Santa Fe, New Mexico 87504
(505) 827-2444

Department of Social Services
Day Care Unit
40 North Pearl Street/33 Broadway, 1st Floor
Albany, New York 12243
(800) 342-3715 ext. 432-2763

Child Care Section
Division of Facility Services
701 Barbour Drive
Raleigh, North Carolina 27603
(919) 733-4801

Department of Human Services
Child and Family Services
State Capital Building
Bismark, North Dakota 58505
(701) 224-2316

Bureau of Licensing and Standards
30 East Broad Street, 30th Floor
Columbus, Ohio 43215
(614) 466-3438

Department of Public Welfare
P.O. Box 25352
Oklahoma City, Oklahoma 73125
(405) 521-3561

Department of Human Resources
198 Commercial Street, S.E.
Salem, Oregon 97310
(503) 378-3178

Department of Public Welfare
Day Care Services
Health and Welfare Building, Room 529
Harrisburg, Pennsylvania 17120
(717) 466-3438

Department for Children and their Families
610 Mt. Pleasant Avenue
Building 10
Providence, Rhode Island 02908

Department of Social Services
Licensing Unit
P.O. Box 1520
Columbia, South Carolina 29202-1520
(803) 734-5750

Department of Social Services
Child Protection Services
Richard F. Kneip Building
700 Governor's Drive
Pierre, South Dakota 57501
(605) 773-3227

Department of Human Services
400 Deaderick Street
Citizen's Plaza Building
Nashville, Tennessee 37219
(615) 741-3312

Department of Human Services
P.O. Box 2960
Austin, Texas 78769
(512) 450-3260

Division of Family Services
P.O. Box 4500
Salt Lake City, Utah 84110
(801) 538-4100

Department of Social and Rehabilitation Services
103 South Main Street
Waterbury, Vermont 05676
(802) 241-2158

Department of Human Services
Barbez Plaza South
St. Thomas, Virgin Islands 00801
(809) 774-0930

Department of Social and Health Services
State Office Building #2
Mail Stop OB-41
Olympia, Washington 98504
(206) 586-6066

Department of Human Services
1900 Washington Street East
Charleston, West Virginia
(304) 348-7980

Division of Community Services
1 West Wilson Street
Madison, Wisconsin 53702
(608) 266-8200

Division of Public Assistance and Social Services
Hathway Building
Cheyenne, Wyoming 82002
(307) 777-7561

APPENDIX B:
SAMPLE OPERATING BUDGET OF A CHILD CARE CENTER FOR INFANTS AND TODDLERS

(Figures are for one year operation of center for 45 children)

<u>Salaries</u>
Educational Staff

Director/Teacher		$23,000
2 Teachers @$17,000		34,000
2 Assistants @$12,000		24,000
1 Aide @$10,000		10,000
	Subtotal	91,000
	Fringe 17%	15,470
	Total	$106,470
Substitutes (part time/hourly)		2,000
Secretary (part time/hourly)		7,000
Cook (part time-hourly)		8,000
	Subtotal	17,000
	Fringe 17%	2,890
	Total	$19,890
	Total Staff	$126,360

Food (1 meal, 2 snacks/child/day.)..8,000
Toys, crafts, books, educational materials..2,500
Conference Fees...300
Supplies
  Disposables (paper plates, towels, etc.)..350
  Maintenance - cleaning...250
  Office...250
  Medical..75
  Kitchen..200
Other Expenses
  Postage...250
  Insurance..4,000
  Printing...1,000
Rent (1,500 sq. Ft. @approximately $20/sq. ft.)..............................30,000
Utilities (heat, telephone, electricity)...5,000
                                                       Total.....................$52,175

                                        TOTAL..................$169,182

APPENDIX C:
SAMPLE OPERATING BUDGET
OF A CHILD CARE CENTER
FOR PRESCHOOLERS

(Figures are for one year operation of center for 20 children)

<u>Salaries</u>
Educational Staff

Director/Teacher		$23,000
2 Teachers @$17,000		34,000
2 Assistants @$12,000		24,000
	Subtotal	81,000
	Fringe 17%	<u>13,777</u>
	Total	$94,777
Substitutes (part time/hourly)		5,000
Secretary (part time/hourly)		7,000
Cook (part time-hourly)		<u>7,000</u>
	Subtotal	19,000
	Fringe 17%	<u>3,230</u>
	Total	$22,230
	Total Staff	$117,007

Food (1 meal, 2 snacks/child/day.)..31,500
Toys, crafts, books, educational materials..............................8,400
Conference Fees..360
Supplies
  Disposables (paper plates, towels, etc.)..............................600
  Maintenance - cleaning..600
  Office...600
  Medical..125
  Kitchen..200
Other Expenses
  Postage...500
  Insurance...5,000
  Printing..1,500
Rent (2,000 sq. Ft. @approximately $20/sq. ft.)..............40,000
Utilities (heat, telephone, electricity)..............................6,000
                                        Total.................$95,385

                                       TOTAL...............$221,745

APPENDIX D:
CHILD CARE
TAX CREDIT GUIDE

The federal tax credit ranges between 20 and 30 percent of qualified child care expenses. The actual percentage depends on adjusted gross family income (AGI). Families with an AGI of less than $10,000 may qualify for the full amount of the credit, which is 30 percent of expenses up to a maximum of $720 if parents have one child under 15 and $1,440 if they have two or more children under 15. To get a maximum credit, a family must pay at least $2,400 if they have one child and $4,800 if the have two or more children.

Following is a chart of AGIs, percentage applicable, and maximum amount of the credit:

Adjusted Gross Income	Applicable Percentage	Maximum Credits One Qualifying	Two or More Individuals
Up to $10,000	30%	$720	$1,440
$10,001– 12,000	29%	696	1,392
12,001– 14,000	28%	672	1,344
14,001– 16,000	27%	648	1,296
16,001– 18,000	26%	624	1,248
18,001– 20,000	25%	600	1,200
20,001– 22,000	24%	576	1,152
22,001– 24,000	23%	552	1,104
24,001– 26,000	22%	528	1,056
26,001– 28,000	21%	504	1,008
28,001 and over	20%	480	960

To be eligible for the credit parents must be employed or actively looking for employment. The child care expenses claimed cannot exceed the lower earning spouse's income or the income of a single parent. If one spouse is a student or disabled, the expenses claimed (from which the credit is calculated) cannot be more than $200 per month if one child is in care ($2,400 per year) and $400 per month if there are two or more children ($4,800).

Expenses apply to care in a child care center, family day care home, and in the child's own home, if the care is needed to enable parents to work. Transportation fees do not qualify. Payments to dependents (for example, older children caring for younger children) do not qualify; however, payments to relatives who are self-employed or who work for a provider organization do apply. Parents should retain receipts for expenses.

APPENDIX E: ORGANIZATIONS

Administration of Children, Youth and Families
Department of Health and Human Services
Public Health Service
Health Services Administration
Office of Human Development
Washington, D.C.

Conducts research projects. Offers many free pamphlets on issues such as breast feeding, child sexual abuse.

Alliance for Better Child Care (ABC). Contact Children's Defence Fund (see below).

Coalition of more than 50 national organizations. Goal of drafting and promoting federal legislation for comprehensive, long-range child care initiatives.

American Council of Nanny Schools
Delta College
University Center, MI 48710
Joy Sheton, Chairperson

Nonprofit corporation of accredited schools promoting national standards and advocacy for nannies.

Association of Junior Leagues
825 Third Avenue
New York, NY 10022
Sally Orr, Director of Public Policy

The association represents approximately 300 Junior Leagues that are actively involved in developing child care initiatives throughout the country.

Bananas, Inc.
6501 Telegraph Hill
Oakland, CA 94609
Arlyce Currie

Information, consultation, technical assistance in establishing employment-related child care programs. Publications.

Bank Street College of Education
Work and Family Life Studies
610 West 112th Street
New York, NY 10025
Ellen Galinsky, Project Director

Conducts research on work and family issues, advises corporations, conducts parenting workshops. Employee newsletter.

Buck Consultants
500 Plaza Drive
Harmon Meadow, NJ 07096-1533
Barbara Adolf, Associate Benefit Consultant, Dependent Care; John Haslinger, Director of Flexible Benefits

Child care and elder care feasibility studies, employee and employer seminars, development of dependent care benefits, booklets, audio-visuals. Development of flexible benefit plans.

Catalyst
250 Park Avenue South
New York, NY 10003
Dr. Phyllis Silverman, Senior Program Advisor

Publications, technical assistance and research on work and family issues.

Child Care Action Campaign
99 Hudson Street, Suite 1233
New York, NY 10013
Barbara Reisman, Executive Director

Coalition of child care experts and business leaders. Goal is to develop quality, affordable child care in the United States. Offers publications, newsletter, media kit.

Child Care Law Center
625 Market Street, Suite 915
San Francisco, CA 94105
Ms. Abby Cohen, Managing Attorney

Nonprofit organization that provides legal assistance to child care programs, government. Also provides publications on legal issues relating to child care.

Child Care Systems
329 West Main Street
Lansdale, PA 19446
Tyler Phillips, President

Provides nationwide resource and referral to corporations and government. Develops initiatives to respond to local concerns.

Child Welfare League of America
440 First Street, N.W.
Washington, D.C. 20001-2085

Provides information about child care issues.

Children's Defense Fund
122 C Street, N.W.
Washington, D.C. 20001
Helen Blank, Executive Director

Private nonprofit national organization to educate the United States to the needs of children. Provides technical assistance and support to state and local child advocates.

Conference Board
845 Third Avenue
New York, NY 10022
Dana Friedman, Senior Research Fellow
Work and Family Information Center

Provides studies on family related issues, conferences, publications.

Council of Labor Union Women (CLUW)
15 Union Square
New York, NY 10003
Joyce Miller, Director

Promotes resolution of work/family issues, education, technical assistance.

Family Resource Coalition
230 North Michigan Avenue, Suite 1625
Chicago, IL 60601
Bernice Weissbourd, President

National organization promoting groups that help families. Offers publications, newsletter, conferences.

Human Services Risk Management Exchange
5555 North Lamar, Suite K-123
Austin, TX 78751
Jim Strictland

Training and publications in risk management for human resource and child care specialists.

National Adoption Exchange
1218 Chestnut Street
Philadelphia, PA 19107

Publications, research and education to affect public policy on adoption. Monthly newsletter.

National Association for the Education of Young Children
1834 Connecticut Avenue, N.W.
Washington, D.C. 20009
Marilyn Smith, Executive Director

Association of professionals offering publications, resources, conferences on all issues affecting quality child care. Developed a child care credential for training and identifying high-quality child care programs.

National Association for Family Day Care
815 15 Street, N.W.
Washington, D.C. 20005
Sandy Gellert, President

Membership organization for family day care networks. Advocacy, support, and information.

National Association of Hospital Affiliated Child Care Programs
11 N. Batavia Avenue
Batavia, IL 60510
Hanna Sampson, Membership

Supports and promotes hospital child care programs. Membership organized on a regional basis.

National Black Child Development Institute
1463 Rhode Island Avenue, N.W.
Washington, D.C. 20005

Membership organization for agencies serving black child care providers. Research and information.

National Center for Education in Maternal and Child Health
38th and R Streets, N.W.
Washington, D.C. 20057
Robert Baumiller and Rochelle Mayer, Directors

Clearinghouse for information about prenatal care, childbirth education, child health, etc. Extensive publications list.

National Coalition for Campus Child Care
Pam Boulton, Chair
Director, University of Wisconsin-Milwaukee Day Care Center
P.O. Box 413
Milwaukee, WI 53201

Supports and collects data on university child care centers.

New Ways to Work
149 Ninth Street
San Francisco, CA 94103
Barney Olmstead, Suzanne Smith

Information and resources on flexible work schedules, job sharing, etc. Publications.

Parenting Press
7750 31st Avenue, NE
Seattle, WA 98115

Practical publications for parents.

Resources for Child Care Management
109 Mount Airy Road
Bernardsville, NJ 07924

Develops and manages on-site child care centers, provides technical assistance to corporations, conducts conferences, and offers publications.

SUMMA Associates
535 Fremont Drive
Pasadena, CA 91103
Sandra Burud

Develops and manages child care centers, conducts needs assessments. Offices in Boston, Arizona, and California.

Wellesley College
Center for Research on Women
Wellesley, MA 02181
School-Age Child Care Project (SACC)

Research on family and work. School-Age Project provides information and technical assistance to develop programs. Publications.

Work/Family Directions
200 The Riverway
Boston, MA 12215
Gwen Morgan and Fran Rodgers, Codirectors

Provides nationwide resource and referral to corporations, government. Develops materials and initiatives to expand child care throughout the United States.

Yale Bush Center in Child Development and Social Policy
Infant Care Leave Project
Box 11A, Yale Station
New Haven, CT 06520
Edward Zigler, Director

Research on child care options for working parents. Publications.

SELECTED BIBLIOGRAPHY

ALTERNATIVE WORK OPTIONS

"Alternative Work Schedules Becoming More Favorable." *Employee Benefit Pension Review Research Reports*, September 5, 1986, p. 4.
Bureau of National Affairs. "Workplace Alternatives: New Patterns for Working Parents." *Fair Employment Practices*, October 30, 1986, p. 130.
Christensen, Kathleen. "A National Study of Home-Based Work." *Business Link*, Vol. 3, No. 1, p. 8.
"Flexible Work Schedules and Staffing Increase." *Spencer's Research Reports*, August 21, 1987, p. 4.
Kotlowitz, Alex. "Working At Home While Caring for Child Sounds Fine—In Theory." *The Wall Street Journal*, March 30, 1987, p. 21.
New Ways to Work. *The 1987 Selected Annotated Bibliography on Work Time Options*. San Francisco: New Ways to Work.
U.S. Department of Labor, Women's Bureau. *Facts on U.S. Working Women: Alternative Work Patterns*. Fact Sheet No. 86-3. Washington, D.C.: U.S. Department of Labor, Women's Bureau, August 1986.

CHILD CARE INSURANCE

Child, Inc. *Handle With Care: How to Reduce Liability Risks in Programs That Serve Children*. Austin, Tex.: Child, Inc.
Koppelman, Jane. *Child Care Insurance Crisis: Strategies for Survival*. Alexandria, Va.: Capital Publications, Inc., 1986.

EMPLOYER-SUPPORTED CHILD CARE

Adolf, Barbara, and Karol Rose. *Child Care and the Working Parent: First Steps Toward Employer-Involvement in Child Care.* New York: Children At Work, Inc., 1983.

Adolf, Barbara, and Karol Rose. "Child Care: Perceiving the Need, Delivering the Options." *Personnel Journal,* June 1986, pp. 57–65.

AFL–CIO. "Child Care: Slow Progress, Pitiful Funding," Report #3, *Work and Family: Essentials of a Decent Life,* February 21, 1986, pp. 6–14.

Auerbach, Judith D. *In the Business of Child Care: Employer Initiatives and Working Women.* New York: Praeger, 1988.

Bernstein, Aaron. "Business Starts Tailoring Itself to Suit Working Women." *Business Week,* October 6, 1986, pp. 50–54.

Bureau of National Affairs. *Special Survey Report: Child Care Assistance Programs.* Washington, DC: Bureau of National Affairs, March 26, 1987.

Bureau of National Affairs. *Work and Family: A Changing Dynamic.* Washington, DC: Bureau of National Affairs, 1987.

Burud, Sandra L., Pamela R. Aschbacher, and Jacqueline McCrosky. *Employer-Supported Child Care.* Boston: Auburn House, 1984.

California Resource and Referral Network. "Developer's Guide to Child Care." San Francisco: California Resource and Referral Network, 1986.

Catalyst Career and Family Center. *Child Care Information Service: An Option for Employer Support of Child Care.* Position Paper. New York: Catalyst Career and Family Center, 1982.

Chapman, Fern Schumer. "Executive Guilt: Who's Taking Care of the Children." *Fortune,* February 19, 1987, pp. 30–37.

"Child Care: Employer Involvement Potential Explored." *Spencer's Research Reports,* December 1986, 007.6–19.

Collins, Glenn. "Day Care Finds Corporate Help." *New York Times,* January 5, 1987, p. B5.

Dawson, Ann Gilman, Cynthia Sirk Mikel, Cheryl S. Lorenz, and Joel King. *An Experimental Study of the Effects of Employer-Sponsored Child Care Services on Selected Employee Behaviors.* Chicago: Foundation for Human Services, Inc., August 6, 1984.

Densford, Lynn E. "Make Room for Baby: The Employer's Role in Solving the Day Care Dilemma." *Employee Benefit News,* May/June 1987, p. 19.

Dilks, Carol, and Nancy L. Croft. "Child Care: Your Baby?" *Nation's Business,* December 1986, pp. 16–22.

Elder, Janet. "New Focus on Day Care: Children With Sniffles." *New York Times,* May 6, 1987, p. C1.

Emlen, Arthur C. "Does Child Care Affect Employee Productivity?" *Business Link,* Summer 1986, p. 5.

Emlen, Arthur C., and Paul E. Koren. *Hard to Find and Difficult to Manage: The Effects of Child Care on the Workplace.* Portland, Oreg.: Regional Research Institute, Portland State University, 1984.

Friedman, Dana. *Corporate Financial Assistance for Child Care.* New York: Conference Board, 1985.

Friedman, Dana. *Family-Supportive Policies: The Corporate Decision-Making Process.* New York: The Conference Board, 1987.

Friedman, Dana. *Government Initiatives to Encourage Employer-Supported Child Care*. New York: Center for Advocacy Research, 1983.

Friedman, Dana. "Special Report: Child Care for Employees' Kids." *Harvard Business Review*, March–April 1986, p. 12.

Galinsky, Ellen. "Investing in Quality Child Care." A Report for AT&T, November 1986.

Garfield, Eugene. *Current Comments—Child Care: An Investment in the Future. Part 3. Corporate-sponsored Child Care Is More than Just Baby-sitting*. Philadelphia: Institute for Scientific Information, 1986.

Herr, Judy, Karen Zimmermann, Margaret Saienga. "National Child Care Study." University of Wisconsin, Stout, Menomonie, Wisconsin. Published in *Child Care Center*, January 1987, pp. 18–19; May 1987, pp. 46–47.

Jensen, Rita Henley. "Perks: When High Salaries Aren't Enough." *The National Law Journal*, June 22, 1987, p. 30.

Kamerman, Sheila B. *Meeting Family Needs: The Corporate Response*. New York: Pergamon Press, 1984.

Kamerman, Sheila B., and Alfred J. Kahn. *The Responsive Workplace: Employers and a Changing Labor Force*. New York: Columbia University Press, 1987.

Lydenberg, Steven D. "Child Care Update: Business Takes First Real Steps." *Council on Economic Priorities Newsletter*. Publication N86-11, New York: Council on Economic Priorities, November 1986.

McQueen, Michel. "States Set Pace on Innovative Laws for Child Care, Parental Leaves, Women's Pay Equity Standards." *The Wall Street Journal*, October 1, 1987, p. 72.

Morgan, Elizabeth L., and Diane Hawk Spearly. *Child Care Consortiums by Employers: Four Interorganizational Issues to Consider When Developing a Joint Project*. OHDS/ACYF Grant #90CW670/01, U.S. Department of Health and Human Services. Austin, Texas: Austin Child Guidance and Evaluation Center.

O'Brian, Penny. *How to Select the Best Child Care Option for Your Employees*. Binghamton, N.Y.: Almar Press, 1987.

Policy/Action Institute. *Corporate Child Care Initiatives: The Potential for Employer Involvement in Child Care Programs*. Boston: TEE, Inc., 1986.

St. Paul Chamber of Commerce Child Care Task Force. *Sick Child Care Dilemma: Solutions for Business*. St. Paul: St. Paul Chamber of Commerce Child Care Task Force, August 1986.

Wallace, Claudia. "The Child Care Dilemma." *Time*, June 22, 1987, pp. 54–60.

"Worksite Child Care Centers: Experiences of Eight Workplace Centers Summarized." *Spencer's Research Reports*, August 1987, .007.6–9.

PREGNANCY AND PARENTAL LEAVE

American Academy of Pediatrics. *Health in Day Care: A Manual for Health Professionals*. Elk Grove Village, Ill.: American Academy of Pediatrics, 1987.

Catalyst, Inc. *Corporate Guide to Parental Leaves*. New York: Catalyst, Inc.

"Pregnancy and Employment: Problems and Progress." *Fair Employment Practices*, Bureau of National Affairs, August 20, 1987, p. 101.

"Pregnancy Leave Practices." *Fair Employment Practices*, Bureau of National Affairs, June 25, 1987, p. 78.

"Prenatal Program: Healthy Births and Bottom Lines." *Employee Benefit Plan Review*, October 1987, pp. 44–48.

U.S. Bureau of National Affairs. *Pregnancy and Employment*. Washington, D.C.: Bureau of National Affairs, 1987.

Washington Business Group on Health. "Promoting Prenatal Health in the Workplace," Washington, D.C.: Washington Business Group on Health, November 1986.

QUALITY CHILD CARE

Berrueta-Clement, John R., Lawrence J. Schweinhart, W. Steven Barnett, and Sue Bredekamp, Editors. *Developmentally Appropriate Practice*. Washington, D.C.: National Association for the Education of Young Children, 1986.

Collins, Glenn. "Latchkey Children: A New Profile Emerges." *The New York Times*, October 14, 1987, p. C1.

Divine-Hawkins, Patricia. *National Day Care Home Study Final Report, Executive Summary, Family Day Care in the United States*. Washington, D.C.: U.S. Department of Health and Human Services, Publication No. (OHDS)80–3–287, 1983.

Epstein, Ann S., and David P. Weikart. *Changed Lives: The Effects of the Perry Preschool Program on Youths Through Age 19*. Ypsilanti, Mich.: High Scope Press, 1984.

Fredericks, Beth, Robin Hardman, Gwen Morgan, and Fran Rodgers. *A Little Bit Under the Weather: A Look at Care for Mildly Ill Children*. Boston: Work/Family Directions, 1986.

Hofferth, Sandra L., and Deborah A. Phillips. "Child Care in the United States 1970 to 1995." *Journal of Marriage and the Family*. Vol. 49, August 1987, pp. 559–571.

Lawrence, Merle, Project Director. *California Child Care Initiative Year-End Report*. San Francisco: California Resource and Referral Network, January 1987.

Long, Lynette, and Thomas Long. *The Handbook for Latchkey Children and Their Parents*. New York: Arbor House, 1983.

Modigliani, Kathy, Marianne Reiff, and Sylvia Jones. *Opening Your Door to Children: How to Start a Family Day Care Program*. Washington, D.C.: National Association for the Education of Young Children, 1987.

Phillips, Deborah A., Editor. *Quality in Child Care: What Does Research Tell Us?* Washington, D.C.: National Association for the Education of Young Children, 1987.

Roupp, Richard. *Children at the Center: Final Report of the National Day Care Study. Executive Summary*. Cambridge, Mass.: ABT Associates, 1979.

Save the Children, Southern States Office. *Family Day Care: An Option for Rural Communities*. Atlanta, Ga.: Save the Children, Southern States Office, OHDS Grant #90 PD 86567/01.

U.S. Bureau of the Census. *After-School Care of School-Age Children: December 1984*. Current Population Report, Series P-23, No. 149, Washington, D.C.

U.S. Bureau of the Census. *Who's Minding the Kids? Child Care Arrangements: Winter 1984–85*. Current Population Reports, Series P-70 No. 9. Washington, D.C.: Bureau of the Census.

WORK AND PARENTING

Burden, Diane S., and Bradley Googins. *Balancing Job and Home-Life Study*. Boston: Boston University School of Social Work, 1985.

Catalyst Career and Family Center. *Corporations and Two Career Families: Directions for the Future*. New York: Catalyst, Inc., 1982.

Crouter, Ann C., Ted L. Houston, Susan M. McHale, and Maureen Perry-Jenkins. "Processes Underlying Father Involvement in Dual-Earner and Single-Earner Families." *Developmental Psychology*, Vol. 23, No. 3,000–000, American Psychological Association (1987).

Day Care Information Service. "Welfare Reform, The Issue for 1987, Part II: Action in the States and Washington, DC." *Day Care Information Service Special Reports*, Vol. 16, No. 6, March 2, 1987.

Fernandaz, John P. *Child Care and Corporate Productivity: Resolving Family/Work Conflicts*. Lexington, Mass.: Lexington Books, 1986.

Galinsky, Ellen, and Diane Hughes. *Fortune Magazine Child Care Study*. New York: Bank Street College of Education, 1986.

Galinsky, Ellen, Diane Hughes, and Marybeth Shinn. *Work and Family Life Study*. New York: Bank Street College of Education, 1986.

Harris, Louis, and Associates, Inc. *American Family Report, 1980–81, Families at Work: Strengths and Strains*. Survey. Minneapolis: General Mills Inc., 1981.

Kamerman, Sheila B. *Parenting in an Unresponsive Society: Managing Work and Family Life*. New York: Free Press, 1980.

Magid, Renee. *When Mothers and Fathers Work: Creative Strategies for Balancing Career and Family*. New York: Amacon, 1987.

"National Survey: Americans Call for Child Care." *Ms.*, March 1987, p. 44.

New York State School of Industrial and Labor Relations. "Working Parents." *ILR Report*, New York State School of Industrial and Labor Relations, Cornell University, Fall 1987.

O'Connell, Martin and David E. Bloom. *Juggling Jobs and Babies: America's Child Care Challenge*. Washington, D.C.: Population Reference Bureau, Inc., Number 12, February 1987.

"Work and Family." *Personnel Administrator*, August 1987, pp. 36–79.

Periodicals

Business Link: The Report on Management Initiatives for Working Parents
Resources for Child Care Management
P.O. Box 672
Bernardsville, NJ 07924
Quarterly, $30/year.

Child Care Center
Lake Publishing Company
17730 West Peterson Road
Box 159
Libertyville, IL 60048–0159
Bimonthly. No charge for child care center managers; all others, $30/year.

Child Care Information Exchange
17916 NE 103rd Ct.
Redmond, WA 98052
For child care center directors. Bimonthly, $25/year.

Day Care USA: Day Care Information Service
United Communications Groups
4550 Montgomery Avenue, Suite 700 N
Bethesda, MD 20814
Biweekly, $163/year.

Labor Relations Today
U.S. Department of Labor
Bureau of Labor Management
Relations and Cooperative Programs
Room N5–419 Frances Perkins Building
200 Constitution Ave., N.W.
Washington, D.C. 20210
Bimonthly, free.

National Report on Work & Family
Buraff Publications, Inc.
The Bureau of National Affairs, Inc.
2445 M Street, N.W.
Washington, D.C. 20037
Monthly, $345/year.

Pre-K Today
Scholastic
730 Broadway
New York, NY 10003
Monthly. No charge to center directors.

Work and Family Life: Balancing Job and Personal Responsibilities
Editorial Offices:
Bank Street College of Education
610 West 112 Street
New York, NY 10025
Circulation Offices:
The Newsletter Bureau
55 Wall Street
Norwalk, CT 06850
Monthly. Ordered by employer for employees, price depends on quantity.

INDEX

About the Author

BARBARA ADOLF received a B.S. degree from Cornell University and a Master's degree in education from Bank Street College. She taught children in private nursery schools and public schools, and trained teachers at Kingsborough Community College, Brooklyn College, Kean College, and in day care centers throughout New York City.

In 1981, Ms. Adolf founded Children At Work, Inc., with Karol Rose. For five years, the firm consulted with major corporations throughout the United States on employer-supported child care. In 1986, Ms. Adolf joined Buck Consultants, an international employee benefit and pension actuarial consulting firm, as associate benefit consultant. She continues to consult with corporations across the country on dependent care—child and elder care issues. She is a working mother.